WOMAN
IMAGE OF THE HOLY SPIRIT

WOMAN
IMAGE OF THE HOLY SPIRIT

by
Joan Schaupp

Introduction by
Carroll Stuhlmeuller, C.P.

Library of Congress Cataloging-in-Publication Data

Schaupp, Joan P., 1932-
　　Woman : image of the Holy Spirit / Joan P. Schaupp.
　　　　p. cm.
　　Includes bibliographical references and index.
　　ISBN 1-57309-114-6 (pbk. : alk. paper). -- ISBN 1-57309-115-4
　　(cloth : alk. paper)
　　1. Feminity of God. 2. Holy Spirit. 3. Image of God. 4. Woman
　　(Christian theology) I. Title. II. Series: Catholic Scholars
　　Press (Series)
　　BT153.M6S325　　　1996
　　231'.3--DC20　　　　　　　　　　　　　　　　96-31382
　　　　　　　　　　　　　　　　　　　　　　　　　　CIP

Editorial Inquiries:
International Scholars Publications
7831 Woodmont Avenue, #345
Bethesda, MD 20814

To order: (800) 55-PUBLISH

TABLE OF CONTENTS

PAGE

Oh, morning, at the brown brink eastward, springs—Because the Holy Ghost over the bent *World broods with warm breast and with ah!* bright wings.

—"God's Grandeur"
Gerard Manley Hopkins

INTRODUCTION

The finest compliment for an author is not that the reader's questions are answered but rather that the reader's mind has been stirred into contemplation. Such an author of necessity handles a controversial issue with openness and vigor.

Like the biblical writer Ezekiel, a good author leads us to "the center of the plain" and there summons the dry, dead bones of the past back to life (Ezek ch. 37). In the vision of Ezekiel it was not enough for the spirit of God to fit the bones together and cover them with sinew and new flesh. The body still remained just a corpse standing on its feet. Then the prophet announced the word of God:

From the four winds come, O spirit, and breathe into these slain, that they may come to life.

Mrs. Joan Schaupp likewise does more than fashion beautiful answers, putting all the parts carefully back together again. She breathes new life into us, where we ponder and pray. To accomplish this goal of strenuous, interior reaction, she deals extensively with symbols. By the use of symbols authors respect their readers and model themselves upon the Bible. Ezekiel's vision of dry bones strewn across the open plain is one of many symbolic presentations in his prophecy.

Symbols, according to Thomas Fawcett, ought

to be distinguished from signs. Signs are comparatively simple and direct. They can be arbitrary devices, like traffic lights, red and green, which silently shout "Stop!" or "Go!" Signs also emerge, not just from consensus among people but also from the normal experience of life. For instance, people do not have to agree among themselves that smoke is a sign of fire. However, in both cases signs speak clearly and unequivocably; they call for immediate action. When a red light turns green or when smoke bellows into the sky, no one stops to philosophize but moves at once into action.

Symbols, on the contrary, evoke a serious response of thought and prayer before action can be taken. Symbols are born out of life and carry a multiple significance to other people. They stir up an interior reaction and orientate the attention of many persons upon a single idea. They are born in and for an encounter and normally charge an idea with emotional intensity. For this reason poetry and other art forms abound with symbol.

Born out of life, symbols emerge from the deepest recesses of personality and express what can take even the "parent" by surprise. Symbols carry one's fearsome and most exciting intuitions up to the surface where secrets are communicated with others. The other person responds with contemplation, wonder and enduring prayer. By this thoughtful response, other people are interiorizing the symbol and making it part of their life at its core or pith where mind, will, emotions, memory and hopes all converge.

To express a symbol, then, one must be willing to lay bare one's deepest, private self before others who are then allowed to transform this symbol into themselves!

For a symbol to strike others with such force that it reaches into their deepest self and sustains contemplation, a symbol must be *real* in the one who creates it and expressed *openly* for others to see. The symbols of the Bible begin with reality: Israel was led out of Egypt, through the desert, into the Promised Land. Israel was scattered like dead bones across the plains of exile in Babylon and yet was brought back to life again. Jesus was born, ministered to his fellow Israelites, died and rose from the grave.

Out of such real moments of life, the Bible created its symbols—not "signs" which immediately and directly imparted their message but "symbols" which called for prayer and the interior response of faith.

Mrs. Joan Schaupp reaches into years of prayer within her heart and speaks her symbol of *woman*. The rest of us, men and women, hear an echo of ourselves in her symbolic words. Mrs. Schaupp touches us with gentleness. She does not deaden our intellect and think for us; nor does she shout the answer at us. She stimulates our thoughts, and more than our thoughts, for we must respond with our emotions, memories and hopes. She summons the spirit that breathes new life within us.

Carroll Stuhlmueller, C.P.
The Catholic Theological Union at Chicago

ACKNOWLEDGMENTS

I would like to thank the following people for their generous time, interviews, reference suggestions and manuscript criticisms. Each of them has contributed their time generously at some moment during the development of this book. I would especially like to thank Father Carroll Stuhlmueller and Dr. Joseph Blenkinsopp for their scholarly criticism of my manuscript. If there are any Scriptural errors, in the book, they are due to some extensive re-writing after their final criticisms.

I would also like to thank Marquette University, Milwaukee, Wi., and St. Norbert College, De Pere, Wi., for graciously allowing me to use their libraries.

And I would like to thank my husband and my children for their emotional support and patience during the three years I researched and wrote this book.

Dr. Joseph Blenkinsopp: Hebrew scholar, Notre Dame University, Notre, Dame, Ind.

Rod Brownfield: Editor, Pflaum-Standard, Dayton, Ohio.

Rev. Max Cala, O. Praem.: Director, Meditation Center, St. Norbert Abbey, De Pere, Wi.

Sister Lorraine Cann, SSND: Adult education consultant, family life education, Diocese of Green Bay.

Rev. Geofrey Claridge, O. Praem.: Archivist, St. Norbert Abbey, De Pere, Wi.

Dr. J. Massingberd Ford: Associate professor of theology, leave of absence, Notre Dame University, Notre Dame, Ind.

Rev. Joel Garner, O. Praem.: Director, Theological Institute, St. Norbert College, De Pere, Wi.

Rev. Thomas Golden: Pastor, St. Francis Xavier, De Pere.

Dr. Monika Hellwig: Department of Theology, Georgetown University, Washington, D.C.

Rev. George Maloney, SJ: Director, John XXIII Institute for Eastern Studies, Fordham University, New York City.

Sister Marie Gertrude Mlodzik, OP: Adult education consultant, department of religious education, Diocese of Green Bay.

Tere and Jim Scully: Dove Publications, Pecos, New Mexico.

Brother David Steindl-Rast, OSB: Co-director, Center for Spiritual Studies, Fairfield, Conn.

Rev. Carroll Stuhlmueller, CP: Hebrew and Scripture professor, Catholic Theological Union at Chicago and St. John's University, New York City.

Rev. Michael van der Peet, SCJ: Director, St. Joseph House of
Prayer, Milwaukee, Wi.
Mary Lou Ziga: Director, St. Catherine Library and Book
Shop, Green Bay, Wi.

I would also like to thank my prayer communities, the
many people who prayed with me during the growth and
development of this book.

11

AUTHOR'S PREFACE

Woman, Image of the Holy Spirit is not a statement of theological certitude. Rather, it's an intuition, a statement of the heart about my inner self, my being. It's an attempt to answer a question too long unarticulated by theologians and philosophers: "How is woman equal with man in the image of God?"

Since the 60's American society has been in an uproar as women everywhere seek their rightful place. All during this turmoil it has been apparent to me the woman's movement is a scream of rage for self identity. Most women really aren't sure of themselves as "made in the image and likeness of God" in a society that has pictorialized God as all male.

In this outcry we women are asking, "Are we only mini males as much of western psychology has drummed into us? Or is there more to woman than western society has admitted?"

"Is there more to God than western society has recognized?" As the Anglican Scripture scholar and minister, J. B. Phillips, has asked, "Is our God too small?"

All during this tumultuous period of women's lib I've been very secure in my own sense of identity as made in the image of God. I found my own answer in a very basic text, Genesis 1:26-27:.

Then God said: *Let us make man in our image, after our likeness . . . male and female he created them.*

13

This simple statement was a personal revelation several years ago. It said to me (no matter what our theological texts state) that God is more than merely all male, for both male and female together are in his image. As Dr. J. Massingberd Ford writes in *The Spirit and the Human Person:* "Neither man alone nor woman alone can wholly reflect the Deity, but the harmony of the best qualities in both man and woman can reflect some of God's radiance."

For some reason most Christian theologians have missed this very obvious and basic fact in Scripture, that male and female together are in the image and likeness of God. It is a tragic fact of history, that many of our Christian theologians and teachers have thought of the male *only* as being in the image of God.

But how are women in the image and likeness of God? This is a basic question that needs more attention. My own intuition, formed by my meditation on Scripture, tells me I am patterned after the Holy Spirit.

I haven't discovered this deepest meaning of myself in any classroom or political gathering. The thought has come to me most powerfully when I'm in prayer. I've found myself in quiet moments by a waterfall and in prayer groups clasping hands with friends as we chant, "Jesus, Jesus, Jesus." More importantly, I've discovered the meaning of myself as *woman* in deep, meditative moments with the Bible, especially in the Books of Wisdom.

All during these quiet moments this "voice" within keeps insisting that I, a woman, *am* in the image of God in my very femininity, more specifically in the image of the Holy Spirit.

Perhaps there is a danger in this point of view: of polytheizing God, of turning the Holy Spirit into a woman, of twisting the processions within the Trinity into biological generation. This is theological error. But according to the Hebrew scholar, the Rev. Carroll Stuhlmueller, C.P., this danger of turning God into a woman is no more erroneous than thinking of him only as Father.

The Holy Spirit is a spirit, a person beyond sex, proceeding from both the Father and the Son in a manner that mystifies theologians. Yet there is something prevadingly feminine about the actions of the Holy Spirit. In these actions I perceive a Platonic prototype or great idea for this other person, woman.

I've grown in this thought very slowly, interviewing, just thinking, researching in several midwestern campus libraries. Immersed in this conviction I've chased after the idea in lecture hall and library, asking every authority who has wandered into this Green Bay Diocese his or her opinion on the subject.

Encouraged onward by theologians, Scripture scholars, book publishers and librarians, I've tracked down the idea, only to discover I'm not the first. The German theologian, Matthias Scheeben, hinted at it, so did the Carmelite nun, Edith Stein. I've found this idea bolstered by the findings in modern Scripture study and the ideas expressed in Jungian psychology. I've been especially encouraged by the seeds of the idea I've discovered hinted at in some of the writings of the early Fathers of the Church.

As this idea has developed I've become very sure that I, as a woman, am in the image of the Holy

Spirit. I've become very comfortable identifying myself with the role of comforter, advocate, counselor, intercessor, helper, principle of love and unity, giver of life. This is the work of the Holy Spirit on the spiritual level. It is also the work of woman in the human sphere.

Although I'm not a professional theologian, philosopher or psychologist, I've grappled with these disciplines in my search for my identity as woman. I've been criticized by some theologians for treading into areas where I'm not an expert. But others who've read this manuscript, or parts of it, have thanked me for the feminine insights I've given them into the role of the Holy Spirit.

Joan Schaupp
May 18, 1975
(Pentecost Sunday)

One

"A WORTHY IDEA"

The idea, woman is made in the image of the Holy Spirit, has germinated in my mind for several years like a seed buried in the nourishing soil, waiting, through the gentle action of water and time, to finally burst forth. Then, when it gradually began to sprout, I sought encouragement as if for sunlight, turning to others, asking, "What do you think of the notion that woman is made in the image of the Holy Spirit?"

One priest friend, Father James Vanden Hogen, at that time vice-chancellor of the Diocese of Green Bay, was enthusiastic. "It's a beautiful idea. Just keep telling it and telling it," he said. "For too long we've thought of God as all male."

Next, I turned to Sister Lorraine Cann, a consultant for family life education in the Green Bay Diocesan Education Department. When I first met Sister Lorraine she was principal at St. Francis in De Pere, the grade school where our children were enrolled. At that time she was still in the full religious habit of the School Sisters of Notre Dame, garbed in black, hidden behind the veil. She has since emerged as a very attractive, well-groomed woman.

For Sister Lorraine this growth as a religious into full-class citizenship in the Church has been a time of real soul-searching. I realized this when I heard her speak at a Serra meeting in our community on the changing role of the nun and woman in the Church. Her quest for the role of woman and also woman-religious was evident throughout that meeting.

During this forum Sister Lorraine compared woman as symbol of love to the love principle of the Trinity, the Holy Spirit. Later, remembering her lecture, I decided she was the person I should consult first when I began my own quest for a fuller meaning of woman in relation to the Trinity.

Sister Lorraine was most receptive when I discussed my ideas with her, for she had had similar inklings of inspiration herself. "So much that we associate with the Spirit is like woman," she agreed. "The descriptions of the Spirit as helper, comforter, advocate of the Father and the Son . . . the idea of birth through the Spirit, all these are feminine attributes."

Then she smiled a bit, a twinkle breaking at the corner of her eyes as she said, "And the Spirit works indirectly through others and often illogically."

The parallel between the Holy Spirit and woman scared her, Sister Lorraine admitted. In her own meditations on Scripture, she had found this striking relationship between the work of the Spirit and the work of a human mother. "The woman's role is to give life. Women inspire, make the father image appealing. Psychologists tell us boys learn to love the father image through their mother. The mother builds the father image," she said.

"In the family it is the mother who upholds the father's authority, just as the Spirit leads to the Father," she added.

"A Worthy Idea"

Pentecost Sunday, May, 1964

Pentecost Sunday, May, 1964, is the birth date for this long meditation of mine on woman. That Sunday morning while I was praying after Communion a thought flashed into my mind: *I'm made in the image of God, but I'm really not like God, the Father. Nor am I an exact image of Christ . . . Then who am I like? . . . I must be an image of the Holy Spirit . . . for the Spirit is love, gives birth.*

After sharing this thought with my husband, Bob, who seemed visibly impressed, I attempted to express this idea for the first time in a column, "At Home," which I was then writing for the *Green Bay Register.* In an article entitled, "Reflection—Pentecost Sunday," I wrote:

"If man was made in the image and likeness of God, then woman was made in the image and likeness of the Holy Spirit. . . .

"Certainly woman does not reflect God, the Father. God the Father is builder and creator of the universe. His creations are endless. He piles up mountains and tears down valleys. . . . His mind is overflowing with an incredible variety of systems of knowledge and scientific laws, all waiting for man to grasp and understand.

"Man mimics his Creator endlessly. He builds, builds, builds—cities, nations, empires. He organizes endlessly, systems of thought, new philosophies. . . .

"But women are not builders (not in the stone upon stone sense), nor is the Holy Spirit. . . . The Holy Spirit does not build mountains. The Spirit moves people.

". . . And this, in a sense, is the work of woman.

Often, she moves quietly, inspiring others. Her work as mother . . . and as wife is the task of molding others. She helps others to creativity.

". . . Man reflects God, the Father, (or God, the Christ) aspect of the Deity. But what does woman reflect: If man was made in the image and likeness of God, what was woman made in? . . . She must reflect something feminine in the Deity. . . . My intuition tells me she reflects God in His Spirit."

Now that I read over my first thoughts on the Holy Spirit excerpted from that original newspaper column, I feel perhaps I overemphasized the motherly, inspiration qualities of woman and overemphasized the building, knowledge aspects of man. I was stressing differences, rather than likenesses to help prove my point. I am aware that in healthy personality development it is also important to stress the likenesses between the sexes.

Many sociologists argue the difference between men and women in any society is caused by the culture, built into children by their parents and their environment. Yet numerous scientific studies also indicate there are very real biological, physiological and psychological differences between male and female.

All of us interested in human personality must ask whether the cultural differences between men and women observable in most societies are created only by environment or whether they are rooted in some real distinctions between male and female. I am taking this debate one step further, asking: *Do these apparently inherent differences in male and female reflect an essential distinction in the life of God,*

20

within the Trinity?
    I think they do. And I believe I found the key to
this answer on Pentecost Sunday, May, 1964, during
a quiet moment after communion.

The Spirit in the New Testament
    During the summer of 1970 I began copying out
all the references to the Holy Spirit in the New Testament, adding them to a notebook I was then organi-
zing on woman. While first underlining these references and then copying them, my sense of motherly
and archetypal feminine in the Holy Spirit intensi-
fied. I became more and more intrigued, for Scripture
reinforced and expanded my notion of analogy between woman and the Spirit.
    In the New Testament, in various translations,
the Holy Spirit *leads*, is a *helper*, an *intercessor* for
people with God, *makes* the new Christian *a child of
God, gives* spiritual *birth, teaches* the child *to obey*
God, *teaches* the child *to speak* in a new tongue, *gives*
a heart of *love, inspires* to wisdom, *does the will* of
the Father. All these activities I would consider analo-
gous to the work of the mother in the human family.
    The Good News for Modern Man translation
comes closest to portraying the Holy Spirit in a more
feminine manner. Others gloss over this impression,
calling the Spirit *Paraclete, Advocate* and other im-
personal terms. But the *Good News* version in the
Gospel of John calls the Spirit, *Helper*, dramatically
drawing attention to the definition of *woman* in
Genesis 2:18: "a help (for man) like unto himself."
    The following quotations are some of the refer-
ences in the *Good News for Modern Man* translation

21

which suggested to me that the Spirit is in some
mysterious way a pattern for the feminine:

> *... Jesus was filled with joy by the Holy Spirit ..."*
> (*Lk*. 10:21).
> *... No one can enter the Kingdom of God unless he
> is born of water and the Spirit. Flesh gives birth to flesh,
> and Spirit gives birth to Spirit (Jn. 3:5-6).*
> *... What gives life is the Spirit (Jn. 6:63).*
>
> *The Helper, the Holy Spirit whom the Father will
> send in my name, will teach you everything, and make
> you remember all that I have told you (Jn. 14:25).*
>
> *But when the Spirit of truth comes, he will lead you
> into all the truth. He will not speak on his own, but he
> will tell you what he hears, and will speak of things to
> come (Jn. 16:13).*
>
> *... For God has poured out his love into our hearts
> by means of the Holy Spirit, who is God's gift to us
> (Rm. 5:5).*
>
> *Those who are led by God's Spirit are God's sons
> (Rm. 8:14).*
>
> *... The Spirit makes you God's sons, and by the
> Spirit's power we cry to God, 'Father, my Father!' (Rm.
> 8:15).*
>
> *... for the Spirit pleads with God on behalf of his
> people, and in accordance with his will (Rm. 8:26).*
>
> *... the Spirit and the bride say, 'Come!' (Rv.
> 22:17).*

"A Worthy Idea"

Heartened by my task of copying out references
to the Holy Spirit in the New Testament, I began
interviewing more intensely on the subject. One of
the first I discussed my topic with was Sister Marie
Gertrude Mlodzik, a former vice-president of the

Dominican Sisters of Racine, then serving as an adult education consultant in the Religious Education Department of the Diocese of Green Bay.

"I like that idea, that woman is cast in the image of the Holy Spirit. I do think this sharing of the life and breath, which is the work of the Holy Spirit, is the woman's part," she said when I began discussing this thought with her.

The analogy between woman and the Holy Spirit intrigued Sister Marie Gertrude. Admitting this concept was new to her, she agreed after thinking about it for a while, "Most of the things we attribute to the Holy Spirit are the things we also associate with the feminine: life and breath, love and care and concern, all that gives life and love."

I first met Sister Marie Gertrude at a two-day diocesan seminar on prayer she had helped prepare for priests, religious and laity of the diocese. At this meeting she introduced me to the main speaker, Brother David Steindl-Rast, a Benedictine monk who holds his Ph.D in psychology from the University of Vienna.

One of the founders of the prayer movement in the United States, Brother David is co-chairman of the Center for Spiritual Studies at Fairfield, Conn. He is one of the leaders in the movement in the United States which has been opening our Western theology and ways of viewing Christianity to the more mystical thought of the East.

While attending his lecture, I soon realized Brother David's experience and knowledge of the life within the Trinity was profound. Perhaps, I felt, he could give me some insights into the questions I'd been turning over in my mind.

Fortunately, I was able to talk with him later, telling him of my project. "What is woman? What is her relationship to the Trinity? What is she an expression of as an image of God?" I asked.

Brother David didn't answer immediately, since this question has bewildered theologians and all men for centuries. He waited, as if sensing I had more to say. I did, as I answered my own question, "I think woman is a reflection of the Holy Spirit."

Brother David still didn't answer, but his silence was a welcoming silence, as if he were listening to me as a child of God with something important to say to him. So I answered his silence with another question, "Has anyone written on this? Has any theologian?"

"I think you'll find that idea expressed in the Doctors of the Church somewhere," Brother David assured me, after reflecting a moment longer. But he immediately cautioned me that the idea has never really been accepted. "I knew a Dominican who wrote his thesis on that subject in Vienna, but it was rejected," he said.

However, Brother David didn't reject the idea. He thought it had merit, even though not popularly accepted among theologians and scholars in the Church. Perhaps, if he had responded differently, I might have dropped the project right then. But he encouraged me.

I can still see Brother David in my imagination, telling me intently, "I think you should pursue it. I think it's a worthy idea."

Two

RUAH, THE BREATH OF LIFE

The discovery of the grammatically feminine
ruah, which means *breath of life*, or *spirit of God*, a
mighty wind in Hebrew, was the next step in my long
search for the meaning of woman in her relation to
the Holy Spirit.

The noted Hebrew and Scripture scholars,
Carroll Stuhlmueller, C.P., of Catholic Theological
Union, and Notre Dame's Joseph Blenkinsopp, have
since cautioned me that one cannot make the jump
directly from the grammatical feminine to the personified, *She*, in Hebrew. There are other more scholarly
approaches to the subject.

But I made that leap instinctively when Father
Stuhlmueller told me during an interview, "*Ruah*, or
spirit of God in Hebrew, is feminine in its grammatical form."

I can still remember vividly the impression his
statement made on me. *Ruah! That's it. That's the
answer*, I reacted immediately.

This inference of femininity in the *spirit of God*,
hinted at only through a grammatical suggestion in
Genesis, develops more graphically in the later Wisdom literature. Here the Wisdom of God (which can
be associated with the Spirit of God) describes Herself
in imagery strongly reminiscent of Genesis 1 when
She compares Herself in Sirach 24:3 to a "mist cover-

ing the earth."

But this suggestion of femininity in the grammatically feminine gender of *ruah* is not enough to develop a theology of the feminine in the Spirit of God. It is only the first clue.

When I first met Father Stuhlmueller I was on assignment for the diocesan weekly, *The Spirit*, covering his lectures on trends in Biblical studies for a theology series at Sacred Heart Center, Oneida, Wi.

An internationally respected Hebrew scholar, Father Stuhlmueller has written several commentaries on Scripture, contributing to many Biblical journals, including *The Jerome Biblical Commentary*. His understanding of the Hebrew is profound.

During his first lecture here at Oneida I became intrigued by his understanding of the root connotations of Hebrew as he consistently referred to the earliest meanings of the Hebrew words in Scripture. At the first opportunity I asked if I could talk with him about the meaning of the *spirit of God* in Hebrew for a book I was researching on woman. He agreed.

Father Stuhlmueller was noncommital, at first, when I told him I sensed woman was in the image of the Holy Spirit, that I had gleaned this through meditation on Scripture. He never confirmed by opinion during that interview, but all during our conversation he discussed various Hebrew words, such as *mercy, spirit* and *wisdom*, which incorporate femininity right into the Person of God.

He also discussed his impressions of the Israelite tradition of the feminine in God.

Ruah, Breath of Life

During that first interview Father Stuhlmueller explained that the Hebrew word, *ruah*, has a much vaster meaning than *spirit of God*. "It can also mean *roaring wind* or *breath of life*," he said.

These diverse meanings would explain why different translations of the Book of Genesis refer to this *ruah* as a *mighty wind*, the *spirit of God*, or the *breath of God*. My copies of the Bible begin variously in Genesis 1:1-2:

> *In the beginning, when God created the heavens and the earth, the earth was a formless wasteland, and the darkness covered the abyss, while a mightly wind swept over the waters.*

> *In the Beginning of Creation, when God made heaven and earth, the earth was without form and void, with darkness over the face of the abyss, and a mighty wind that swept over the surface of the Waters.*

> *In the beginning God created heaven, and earth. And the earth was void and empty, and darkness was upon the face of the deep. And the spirit of God moved over the waters.*

> *In the beginning God created the heavens and the earth. Now the earth was a formless void, there was darkness over the deep, and God's spirit hovered over the water.*

> *God, at the beginning of time, created heaven and earth. Earth was still an empty waste, and darkness was hung over the deep; but already, over its waters, stirred the breath of God.*

27

When God began creating the heavens and the earth, the earth was at first a shapeless, chaotic mass, with the Spirit of God brooding over the dark vapors.

Each of these translations gives a little different nuance to the ancient Hebrew, *ruah*. Yet, when these texts are read one after another the fullness of the Israelites' sense of the *spirit of God* begins to unfold. They did not refer to a third Person in the Holy Trinity as we Christians now understand the Holy Spirit. Rather, their spirit was an attribute of the one God, the symbol for the spirit of life, a life-giving wind, the principle of life giving breath.

God is both Father and Mother
"Scripturally it isn't entirely correct to think of God only as male. Biblically, God is neither male nor female. Somehow He's both at once," Father Stuhlmueller explained during that first interview. Although modern Scripture scholars generally believe this, teaching God is neither male nor female, God has been pictorialized as all male in our Western Christian culture.

Scripture scholars are beginning to realize that this anthropomorphism of God as only male is incorrect. God is not only Father. He is described in both masculine and feminine terms in the Old Testament.

Sidney Callahan emphasizes this Father-Motherhood of God in *The Illusion of Eve* when she writes, "God is not just 'Father', but 'Mother', too," quoting from Isaiah 66:13:

Like a son comforted by his mother will I comfort you.

28

The essential teaching about God in the Old Testament is that God is One. Yet this unity is a Hebraic or Semitic concept of unity, not the Platonic one of uniformity which has been emphasized in western culture. The Hebraic concept of unity is one more open to diversity, as the many Biblical names for Yahweh indicates.

At one moment during our discussion Father Stuhlmueller warned against this error of consistency of symbol when talking of God. "That was a Greek trait where all the symbols have to fit together," he said.

"In contrast, the Israelites were unafraid of heaping clashing symbols together in one sentence or paragraph, as we see in Chapter 1 of Ezechiel's prophecy," he said.

As he explained, God is repeatedly referred to as the Creator and Father in the Old Testament. But in these books of the Bible various attributes of God are described with feminine imagery. In the Old Testament, the mercy of God is one of these attributes. The very word, *mercy*, in Hebrew is *raham*, a word that also means *womb*. "When God is merciful, this is an image of the mother surrounding the child with warmth, with her life-begetting spirit," he said.

Again in Deuteronomy 33:11 Yahweh is compared to an eagle, like a mother bird, hovering over her nest, very similar to the spirit of God which hovered over creation at the beginning of time: "Like an eagle watching its nest, hovering over its young. . . ."

Father Stuhlmueller continued, "In Isaiah 49:15 the prophet compares God to a mother asking, when

Zion thought it was abandoned, 'Can a mother forget her infant, be without tenderness for the child of her womb?' " (NAB).

"Here God becomes a mother," he said.

Wisdom as the Breath of Yahweh

This attribute of wind, or breath of life, first mentioned in Genesis 1 can be associated with the Wisdom of God which develops as a feminine personification in the sapiential Books of Wisdom. The *Hokmah*, or *Wisdom of God* which gradually evolves in the Wisdom Literature is another form of the feminine which the Israelites incorporated into their God.

It is important to recognize that many of the later Fathers of the Church, especially those in the Alexandrian or Hellenic tradition, identified this Wisdom of the Old Testament with Christ, with the Greek concept of Logos or Word of God. But it is significant for my thesis that three of the very earliest Fathers of the Church, St. Irenaeus of Lyons, Pope St. Clement of Rome and Theophilus of Antioch identified the Spirit of God in the New Testament with the Wisdom texts.

Wisdom, as She evolves in Scripture is obviously a feminine personification. In the sapiential books (Proverbs, Ecclesiastes, Wisdom, Sirach and also some Psalms, Job, Baruch and the Song of Songs) the Israelite scribes gradually developed their concept of wisdom. At first wisdom was a listing of practical sayings, proverbs. Then gradually it was personified in Proverbs 9 as a gracious hostess and in Proverbs 31 as the industrious wife.

In Wisdom 9:4 She emerges as "the consort of Yahweh's throne." Again in Wisdom 7:25 the scribe describes Wisdom as the "breath of Yahweh," identifying Wisdom with the Genesis texts:

She is a breath of the power of God, pure emanation of the glory of the Almighty . . .

In Sirach 24:3-4, in the famous "Eulogy to Wisdom," Wisdom sings Her own praises in a manner traditional in the Middle East a thousand years before Christ. In this eulogy She identifies Herself with the spirit of God hovering over the waters in Genesis 1:2 and the presence of God (the Shekhinah), from earliest Biblical times, manifested by a pillar of cloud (Ex. 16:10). Wisdom says of herself:

I came forth from the mouth of the Most High, and I covered the earth like mist.
I had my tent in the heights, and my throne in a pillar of cloud (Si. 24:3-4).

Wisdom: An Allegory of God

Scripture scholars debate the meaning of the feminine personification of Wisdom developed in the sapiential literature and linked to the spirit of God in both the books of Wisdom and Sirach. Some reject the feminine personification altogether, identifying the Wisdom of the Old Testament with the Word which appears in the New Testament. Others say Wisdom can be identified with the Holy Spirit, but they generally agree this Wisdom is not to be taken literally. She is personified as an allegory.

Scholars agree that throughout her history Israel staunchly maintained her belief in one God. While describing certain characteristics of God, *spirit, wisdom* and *mercy*, with grammatically feminine language and feminine imagery, the ancient Israelites did not consciously separate these attributes from their one true God, whom they frequently envisioned as male.

"Not too much of the feminine characteristics were seen in God, because of the fear of Israel of going along the way of the fertility rites of their neighbors," Father Stuhlmueller said during that first interview. "Worship of these female goddesses were orgies, and Israel over-reacted by making their God almost all male," he said.

The Israelites did not separate the motherly characteristics out of their deity, personifying them in a separate goddess as most of the surrounding civilizations had done. Rather, they embodied the very feminine principles of breath and life, life from the very body of God, the motherhood of their God, into their total concept of their deity.

Their God was One. The unity of God was their great revelation. This God was their Father, but She was also their Mother. God was order and authority, Creator of the universe. But attributes of this God were also described with the grammatically feminine words: *raham, ruah* and *hokmah*.

God was Father. But God was also womb and spirit of life and Wisdom, a "breath of the power of God."

Three

THE BREATH OF GOD AS "HE" IN THE NEW TESTAMENT?

The breath of life imagery used to describe the spirit of God and the Wisdom of God in the Old Testament increases in even greater intensity in the New Testament. It is a continuing development of the concept, *spirit of God*, which first appeared in Genesis as the primeval *ruah*. Only in the New Testament this principle of Spirit becomes separated from the Father, as a distinct person of the Trinity.

Although the personality characteristics of the Holy Spirit in the New Testament appear to be a development of those begun in the spirit of God in the Old, yet, in the Western Church, the Spirit becomes defined with the pronoun, *He*, and is most often thought of as a masculine personality.

Why?

I believe this totally masculine definition is rooted in some of the Manichean and neo-Platonic errors of the time which saw matter as evil or the source of evil and considered woman intrinsically inferior and even evil. After accommodating itself to the popular Hellenism, the Appolonian-reason philosophy of the time, the Western Christian tradition has envisioned God as totally masculine.

The early Fathers of the Church generally agreed that this Spirit in the New Testament was one and the same spirit of God who spoke through the prophets in the Old Testament. Church Councils proclaimed this fact. But the Fathers did not all allocate this Spirit of God in the New with the Wisdom of God which developed in the sapiential books of the Bible.

Many of the Fathers identified this more ancient concept of Wisdom which arose in the Middle East or Sumeria with the then currently fashionable Greek idea of Logos or Word of God. Several of the Fathers, including St. Justin, made the Wisdom of ancient days synonymous with the Word of John's Gospel. Justin followed a tradition established by Philo, the Alexandrian or Hellenic Jew, who identified the Judaic *Wisdom* with the Greek *Word* in the first century, B.C. Those who made Wisdom and the Word synonymous were in the Alexandrian or Hellenic, Platonic school of thought in the Church.

St. Irenaeus and others of the Antiochan school who associated the Spirit of God with Wisdom in the Old Testament were in the Semitic tradition. Their approach to life or philosophy was based more generally on Aramaic thought. According to the patristic scholar George Maloney, S.J., this Semitic approach is more "dynamic, voluntaristic, existential and psychological" in contrast to the Hellenic school which he calls more "static, essential, intellectual, logical."

In his book, *Man the Divine Icon*, Father Maloney describes the intellectual conflict between the two schools as "the opposition between the Semitic approach among the early Christians of encountering God as a total experience of Life and that of the Hellenic, speculative school of Alexandria of meeting God only through intellectual contemplation."

It is the Hellenic school in Christianity which separated the Spirit of God from the earlier, *ruah-hokmah*, breath of life, Wisdom imagery. The Alexandrian Fathers, identifying Hokmah with the Logos, began thinking of the Spirit of God as a third, masculine Person within God. The powerful, feminine, "breath of life" imagery of the Old Testament which had formerly been incorporated into the life of the One God was submerged. Now in the West the feminine in God disappears.

Is This "He" Entirely Correct?

Although we in the Western Church have been accustomed to think of the Spirit as *He*, as masculine, the work of this Third Person of the Trinity which begins at creation intensifies in its motherly giver-of-life qualities in the New Testament. I suspect that more scholars would have considered this Spirit, at least as allegorically feminine, if the texts had been translated from the Aramaic, from the feminine *ruah*, the *breath of life*.

Early in the Church the Fathers began translating the grammatically feminine *ruah* of the Old Testament Aramaic into the Greek, *pneuma*, and the grammatically masculine Latin, *Spiritus Sanctus* or *Holy Spirit*. Partially because of the language problem, the Holy Spirit is now described as *He*.

But is this *He*, which we are now familiar with in our English and Latin translations entirely correct?

I do not believe so, and I hope Scripture scholars and theologians will examine this gender more closely. I base my judgment on the personality characteristics of the Spirit in the New Testament which continue on a line of development from the spirit of God and Wisdom of God in the Old Testament.

The notes to the Gospel of John in *The Jerusalem Bible* confirm my opinion that the Holy Spirit is not an entirely masculine person. They point out that the word for *spirit* in Greek, *pneuma*, is a neuter word. According to the *JB* notes, it is not entirely correct to refer to the Spirit as *He* as we do in our English translations. More properly, in the sense of the Greek, the Spirit would be *It*.

The Anglican Hebrew scholar, Henry Barclay Swete, hints at this question in his classic work, *The Holy Spirit in the Ancient Church*. While writing of certain Aramaic Christian sects' treatment of the Spirit as feminine in the Trinity, Swete states, "It is not of course uncommon to find the Spirit represented as a female in writings of Aramaic origin, the sex being determined by the gender of the Semitic *ruah* or *ruha*."

In this section of his work Swete wonders what our theological treatment of the Spirit would have been if the Scriptures had been handed down in Aramaic, the language of Jesus, rather than in Greek or Latin.

The Spirit as "Mother" Image

The ancient Israelites did not divide their God into three persons. Rather, they incorporated the spirit of God and also the motherhood of God into the very life of Yahweh.

Their words, *ruah* and *raham*, their understanding of the mother aspect of the work of the spirit of God, help explain the Holy Spirit to me. Their root meanings of *ruah* (spirit, breath, roaring wind), *raham* (mercy or womb), and *hokmah* (wisdom) fit in with my intuitive understanding of the actions of the Holy Spirit. It is when we are baptized in the Spirit, literally immersed in the womb of the Spirit, that we receive God's life, becoming children of God, his heirs to the kingdom. As children of God, we are born spiritually of the Spirit. *Ruah* and *raham* symbolize this interior birth to me. The very root meanings of these words, *breath of life* and *womb*, dramatize the meaning of the spiritual rebirth, "to be born of the Spirit."

According to the *Oxford Universal Dictionary*, the term *mother* as a figure of speech, "is applied to things regarded as giving birth, or standing in the relation of a mother, e.g. a condition that gives rise to another, the Church, Nature, one's native country, one's university OE."

It is this kind of mothering I believe applies to the Holy Spirit.

The New Testament consistently describes the actions of the Holy Spirit with this classical dictionary type of birth-giving or mother imagery. In Luke, Chapter 3, John the Baptist predicts one (Christ) will come who will baptize "with the Holy Spirit and Fire." This baptism or immersion in the Spirit predicted by John the Baptist gives rebirth, spiritual birth, just as the mother first gives physical birth to the child.

According to Father Stuhlmueller this allegorical birth imagery is especially true in the Hebrew, since *birth* in this language includes the concepts of caring

37

for, nurturing.

The Good News for Modern Man translation of the New Testament comes closest to describing the work of the Holy Spirit in salvation as a kind of spiritual mothering, of giving rebirth. In Chapter 3 of his Gospel, John the Evangelist describes this spiritual renewal where we find Jesus explaining to Nicodemus the need for a person to "be born again" (Jn. 3:3). Extremely puzzled, Nicodemus asks, "How can a grown person be born again?" (Jn. 3:4).

Jesus answers:

> *I tell you the truth, that no one can enter the Kingdom of God unless he is born of water and the Spirit. Flesh gives birth to flesh and Spirit gives birth to spirit. Do not be surprised because I tell you, 'you must be born again.' The wind blows wherever it wishes; you hear the sound it makes but you do not know where it comes from or where it is going. It is the same with everyone who is born of the Spirit. (Jn. 3:5-8).*

This mother imagery associated with the Spirit threads poetically throughout Paul's epistles. As Paul writes in Romans 8:10, "The Spirit is life for you."

In his letters he writes that the Christian learns to speak "in words taught by the Spirit" (1 Co. 2:13 NAB). The Spirit teaches the Christian to confess, "Jesus is Lord" (1 Co. 12:3). The Spirit makes the person wise and reveals God (Eph. 1:17); unites (Eph. 4:3); gives new birth and new life (Tt. 3:5).

The Spirit is creating a Holy People (1 P. 1:2).

Like any good mother this Holy Spirit unites, gives life, teaches the child to speak, to revere the

Father, instructs about the commandments of the Father. When the child gets in trouble, She is the intercessor, "for the Spirit pleads with God on behalf of His people" (Rm. 8:27).

The Spirit is a universal mother-figure creating a holy people, for "those who are led by God's spirit are God's sons" (Rm. 8:14).

Even though the allegorical mother imagery associated with the Holy Spirit is increasingly vivid in the New Testament, this Person still appears as "wind," just as It first is depicted as a "wind" in Genesis 1. In John 3:8 Jesus compares this Holy Spirit to the wind that "blows wherever it wishes."

Although now giving spiritual birth, bestowing the breath of the life of Yahweh, the Holy Spirit is still a mighty wind, a breath of life, similar to the primeval *ruah*, recorded on Genesis. It is the force that descended on Pentecost,

like a strong wind blowing (*Ac.* 2:2).

Four

THE FEMININE PRINCIPLE IN GOD AS "PUREST SPIRIT"

According to the analytical psychologist, Dr. Erich Neumann, the Holy Spirit of Christianity represents the highest form of the eternal feminine symbolism, the apex of spiritual transformation. In his classical work, *The Great Mother*, he calls the Spirit, "the upper bird of the Great Mother, the dove of the Holy Ghost, the supreme spiritual principle."

The Spirit of God, or *ruah* of the nomadic Israelites, does contain some of the positive, breath-of-life aspects of the Great-Mother idea recognized by many of the world's most primitive tribes as the life force in creation. This Spirit of God is the sharer of life, the breath of life, which permeates all being, gives birth to all creation.

This is the breath of life, active in the very beginning, when God created heaven and earth, . . . and the earth was void and empty with darkness upon the face of the earth. Then the Spirit of God moved out over the waters, as if brooding over the deep.

And life began.

Anthropological studies indicate many of the world's most primitive cultures considered this life-giving aspect of God feminine, often calling it "Mother." Brother David Steindl-Rast tells us of the customs of the Chenchu, a primitive South Central

Indian tribe. These natives, when sitting down to eat the berries or other food they have gathered, take a portion of their food, throwing it back to their mother, their God who is their mother, their source of life.

Sister Marie Gertrude Mlodzik of the Green Bay Diocesan Department of Education says of this notion, "There they understood God as feminine, but somehow we've twisted it around to make God a totally masculine figure."

In the *Art of Loving* the psychoanalyst Erich Fromm writes that research results indicate the very most primitive societies are matriarchal and peace-loving. These primitive cultures generally worship God as mother earth, sensing God as an immanent force that surrounds them, sustaining them in all nature. This cultural sense of deity would correspond to childhood in human development.

Gradually as cultures mature, they move into an adolescent stage of development, rejecting the feminine God, just as teenage boys tend to reject anything "femmy." These societies become patriarchal and God becomes all male. Fromm believes societies and people reach psychological maturity when they move onward again accepting the feminine in God, when they can accept both masculinity and femininity in God.

According to Fromm's viewpoint, a He-She, androgynous God would be a psychologically mature view of the deity.

"The Upper Bird of the Great Mother"
In his book, *The Great Mother*, Dr. Erich

Neumann observes that in the western world the feminine has lost its original archetypal character as goddess. It has been transformed into concept and allegory. Here in the West we recognize the feminine as Ecclesia, Mother Church. At this highest level the feminine is personified allegorically as the Jewish Torah or Hokmah, as Philosophia or Sophia, as Wisdom.

In our Christian tradition, Neumann points out, the feminine vessel of rebirth and transformation becomes Sophia and the Holy Ghost. He calls the heart spring of Sophia, the wisdom of the heart. This is the wisdom of psychic relatedness, not the wisdom of the head.

On a chart in his *The Great Mother*, through a graph of concentric circles, Dr. Neumann contrasts the upper and lower aspects of the Great-Mother idea. On the upper level he places the Holy Spirit, the Church or Ecclesia, Sophia or Wisdom, Mary-Mother of God, eternal life. On the lower level he has the Jaws of Hell, Death, Medea, the negative feminine luring down into death.

Many positive themes of the Great Mother in mythology are themes we Christians consider aspects of the Holy Spirit: rebirth, transformation through surrender and death to self, regeneration through streams of living water, the font of life.

The Great Goddess in its negative aspects is the opposite of the Holy Spirit. In mythology this Great Goddess is often associated with the snake and with orgiastic ritual. Her followers practice temple prostitution and infant sacrifice, are characterized by madness, rage and sexual incest.

Although Neumann does rate the various aspects of the feminine myth as positive and negative, he does not judge them as good or evil. Rather, Jungian psychology recognizes these themes as psychologically true since they consistently re-occur in both myths and dreams.

Scripture also recognizes these two aspects of the feminine. The Bible, however, makes a value judgment. In Proverbs it contrasts Wisdom with Dame Folly; in the prophets, heavenly Jerusalem with wicked Babylon. The Bible consistently warns against feminine evil, against temple prostitution, against all types of orgiastic ritual. In Wisdom 9:13-18, the scribe describes Dame Folly as "acting on impulse," "childish" and "knowing nothing." This Dame Folly apes Wisdom, leads to the valleys of Sheol.

In Christianity, it sometimes appears we are living out some of the most basic themes suggested in mythology. But there is often a perverse difference in pagan mythological themes, as if the myths are a corruption of the truth, aping, mirroring in a distortion the true way to life. While mythological themes often search for this new life through sexual orgy and incest, the message of Scripture is different.

The message of Scripture is the one of spiritual transformation promised by Jesus, "Born of Spirit." It is not a transformation into death, but one into eternal life. This transforming is the work of the Holy Spirit, the Person in the Trinity Neumann calls "the upper bird of the Great Mother, the dove of the Holy Ghost."

The Development in Judaism

Joseph Blenkinsopp points out in his book, *Sexuality and the Christian Tradition*, that the emergence of the celibate and apparently all-male Hebrew God was a most unusual development in religious history, but a necessary one in Judaism. This concept of the all-male God, according to Blenkinsopp, freed these ancient wandering tribes of Israelites from the sexual mysticism, the earth cults, the orgies of their Canaanite neighbors.

According to Blenkinsopp, early Judaism rejected the gods and goddesses of their neighbors, placing their God above the realm of sex. However, popular Judaism never really accepted this celibacy of their God.

Even while the Jewish prophets and priests considered their God almost all male, they recognized the suggestion of feminine archetype in their God from the very beginning, recording it in Genesis 1:26-27:

> *God said, "Let us make man in our image, in the likeness of ourselves...."*
> *(Then) God created man in the image of himself, in the image of God he created him, male and female he created them.*

According to Carroll Stuhlmueller, there is a real problem for the Hebrew scholar in the translation of this passage in Scripture *before* God creates the distinctive sexes. "In Genesis 1:27 this unity of God is generally referred to as *He*, but this isn't entirely correct," he says.

Stuhlmueller believes, "A truer translation would be: 'God created the human race in the image of the godhead, in this divine likeness, male and female created them'."

This God of Genesis 1:27 could just as easily be called, *She* or *Parent*, according to Father Stuhlmueller.

The Immanence of God as Feminine Principle

During my researches on this subject, I was fortunate to interview a priest scholar at St. Norbert College here in De Pere, who prefers to remain anonymous. As with all scholars, he warned me of overemphasis and of dichotomy, of personifying God as either a man or a woman. But he also offered some words of encouragement.

"It is difficult to establish the Holy Spirit as a feminine principle, because God is a spirit. We can not describe a male or female as God," he said.

"However," he added, "most of the view of God and the Trinity has been so put in masculine terms that this emphasis has gone too far. We forget the maternal aspect of God. But the maternal aspect has to be there. There needs to be a lot said about all those qualities of humanity that are considered feminine."

Several aspects of the feminine personality should be considered when we discuss the reality of God, according to this priest scholar. These include the mother's ability to unite the family and put it in order, her power and authority to do this. "The Spirit heals, unites, brings together, gives love. All of those are feminine qualities. We have no right to identify the Spirit in only masculine terms, but It needs to be identified as well in very feminine and human terms," he said.

The quality of woman he believes we have most underplayed in thinking of God is Mary's way of taking events into her heart. "The woman follows the patterns of taking everything into her heart. God ceases to be out there some place, but becomes a deep and personal relationship within the person," he said.

God's way of working through history is an illustration of the feminine inner-relatedness, sense of immanence. "God doesn't come from outside history into history, but comes right in the fabric of history. He came through a geneology recorded in Scriptures. Mary's taking all this into her heart reveals the deeply personal aspect of God in all history and his deep involvement with each individual," he said.

The Feminine Principle in God as Purest Spirit

In his book, *The Seat of Wisdom*, Father Louis Bouyer observes that the religious thought of Judaism, though generally hostile to any idea of sex in God, did recognize something mysteriously feminine in his spirit, *ruah*. Bouyer suggests that the role of *ruah* in Genesis is similar to that of a bird brooding over an egg.

This mysteriously feminine aspect of God becomes Hokmah in the Book of Wisdom, where Dr. Neumann observes the eternal feminine has been transformed from its original archetypal character as goddess into concept and allegory. Through revelation the Hebrew Wisdom is raised above the level of goddess, above the human level onto the plateau, *spirit*. As the scribe writes, "Wisdom is a spirit, a friend to man" (Ws. 1:6).

In chapters 10 and 11 of the Book of Wisdom, Solomon's "consort" of the heavenly throne (Ws. 9:4) emerges as the immanent force within God creating Israel through the periods of her history. She preserved Adam when he was first formed by God, brought him out of sin, giving him power to govern all things. She gave the human race a second term on life by steering Noah to safety. Finally she led the Israelites through the Red Sea, leading them safely through the desert.

Here Wisdom becomes the deeply personal aspect of God in all history. But Wisdom's work as the immanent God is not as an anthropomorphized goddess in human form. Wisdom appears as a tower of flame, a cloud. Wisdom is a Spirit.

Undoubtedly through God's own revelation, Israel reacted, justifiably, against the sexual, ritual excesses of their surrounding neighbors. However, according to Father Stuhlmueller, "Israel never rejected sexuality from the intuition of God, no matter how degrading sex was expressed among the Canaanites."

Instead, the Israelites lifted sex out of orgy, raising it above the weaknesses of the human person. In doing so, Israel incorporated feminine attributes right into God, raised the feminine in God to the level of purest spirit.

In the New American Bible translation this

force, personified allegorically as the consort of the heavenly throne (Ws. 9:4) is described as the "holy spirit of discipline, . . . a kindly spirit, . . . the witness of (God's) inmost self . . ." (Ws. 1:5,6). This "spirit of the Lord" is the "mother" of "all good things" (Ws. 7:11-12); is guided by God (Ws. 7:15); is "an aura of the might of God" (Ws. 7:25).

Also recognizing this trait of wisdom as somehow the feminine archetypal principle, the most ancient Greeks, who preceded the philosophers of the fifth century, B.C., gave their highest honor to Athena. Her temple, the Parthenon on the Acropolis, could be viewed for miles.

Like the Israelites, Wisdom, Athena was not the product of a sex orgy, but sprang from the head of their main god, Zeus, dramatically illustrating the Greek cultural emphasis on the "Mind of God." She was the Athenians' goddess of wisdom, science and warfare, inspiring them to spectacular achievements in science, philosophy and valor.

Similarly these pre-Socratic Greeks recognized that inspiration in some way had a feminine quality, attributing it to the nine Muses, the goddesses of epic poetry, history, lyric poetry, comedy, tragedy, dancing, love poetry, sacred song and astronomy. Ancient authors called on one of the Muses before beginning to write, just as Solomon called on God for the gift of wisdom in his youth: "God of our ancestors, Lord of mercy . . . grant me Wisdom, consort of your throne" (Ws. 9:1,4).

There are similarities between the Greek concepts of Athena, the pagan goddess of Wisdom, and the Hebrew, Hokmah. But there are also inspired differences.

Athena was an aspect of a non-Scriptural Wisdom school which arose in Sumeria around 2500 B.C., spreading throughout the ancient world. Hokmah, which evolves in the Israelite sapiential literature, contains elements of the then world movement, aspects of the Earth Mother, the pagan goddesses. But there are important, inspired differences.

The Jewish scribes added to the world-wide concept of Wisdom. The Hebrew Hokmah is raised above the level of goddess, above the human idolatrous level of god-in-the-image-of-man, to a higher plane, Spirit. Through revelation the ancient Israelites attained a deeper understanding of the feminine principle in God. Never giving this Wisdom human form, they nevertheless recognized Its feminine characteristics, presenting these as concept, as allegory.

The Hebrew revelation raised the feminine principle out of mythology, above the level of "dank, moist, earth, or evil" and lifted it onto the plateau of spirit. This Wisdom is called just that by Solomon:

a spirit . . .
. . . so pure, she pervades and permeates all things. She is
a breath of the power of God, pure emanation of the
glory of the Almighty (*Ws*. 7:1, 24-25).

Five

THE PSYCHOLOGICAL NEED FOR A FEMININE ARCHETYPE IN GOD

There is a very human need to find the feminine in God, to discover ways to express this imagery in human terms without pictorializing God as either male or female. When faced with this lack of healthy imagery, the analytical depth psychiatrist, C. G. Jung, asked, Why has Western Christianity rejected the almost obvious link between Sophia-Wisdom and the Holy Spirit?

A feminine archetype of Wisdom-Holy Spirit would help fill a psychological vacuum of Western civilization.

According to the analytical psychiatry originating with C. G. Jung, it is difficult for both men and woman to achieve psychological integrity without an archetype of the feminine in God. In the Catholic Church the devotion to the Virgin Mary has undoubtedly helped both men and women in their quest for personality wholeness. Mary emerges as that shining figure, that inspiration necessary for both men and women to reach a mature relationship with the Deity.

But Mary is not a part of the Trinity, Western Christianity's dogmatic definition of God. She is the most perfect of all creation in Roman Catholic tradition, the justifiable object of reverence and awe.

51

Mary fulfills our psychological need for feminine imagery in God. But she is not God.

In her book, *The Feminine in Jungian Psychology and in Christian Theology*, Ann Belford Ulanov discusses the need for feminine imagery in our Western concept of the Deity. An associate professor of psychiatry and religion at Union Theological Seminary and a psychotherapist in private practice, Ulanov visualizes adapting Jung's point of view to Christian theology.

During his researches into the human personality, Jung began asking, Why the repression of the feminine in Western culture? Why don't we Western Christians have any femininity in God when human personality cries out for this prototype? Jung wondered why Western Christianity, especially Protestantism, had denied this very basic requirement of the human psyche.

Popular Judaism and popular Catholicism had adapted to this human need by Hypostasizing Wisdom or the Shekhinah (the Hebraic Presence of God) and by almost divinizing Mary. Pious Catholicism has treated Mary as a demi-goddess, as Jung points out, transforming the Trinity into a quasi-quaternity. But Western civilization in its official theology, whether Christian or Judaic, has never accepted the feminine archetype in God.

As an answer to this theological poverty, Jung claimed that the Doctrine of the Assumption, defined by the Roman Catholic Church in 1951, was the most significant religious development in Western civilization since the Reformation.

The Psychological Need for a Feminine
Archetype in God

Does God as All Male Affect the Self Image of Both Men and Women?

The Franciscan sisters, Mary Austin Doherty and Margaret Early, ask several questions about our traditional Christian concept of an all-male God in "Women Theologize," a chapter in *Women in Ministry: A Sisters' View*. Stating, we "need new images of God," they ask, "Is God as male an image which affects a woman's relation and role with respect to men?"

Faculty members at Alverno College, Milwaukee, and associated with the Women's Research Center there, the sisters point out that our theological concepts have all been defined in terms of male experience. Rightfully, they observed, this has had an oppressive influence on women, hindering the development of the woman's image of herself as a full person.

As a solution, the sisters envision a Christian theology balanced with the feminine viewpoint. They consider the work of women theologians, "not a matter of putting feminine patches on a male theology, but of creating a new vision of the future together with the masculine perspective."

Not only women, but men are also crippled by this all-male image of God. To be whole persons, men need to complement their masculine traits with the feminine, according to Erich Fromm. In *The Art of Loving*, Dr. Fromm writes that both men and women need to balance their personalities, developing traits considered typical of the opposite sex.

Fromm rejects as a Freudian error the notion that woman is only an inferior man. "Woman is not a castrated man," Fromm asserts.

If woman is not a castrated man, what is she? It is my opinion that this notion, "castrated man," is a logical result of our "God is male" imagery. Without the feminine in God how can we visualize equality of woman? Or how can we treat as significant the characteristics our culture calls "feminine?"

The Male Need for New Imagery

In trying to solve this problem, I have suggested that the Holy Spirit is the archetype for the feminine in God. Yet Rev. Thomas Golden, pastor of St. Francis Xavier, De Pere, Wi., feels, "This doesn't really solve the problem." In his mind this creates further problems for men in their self image.

"The question is not whether there is femininity in God, but is God loving, tender, merciful," he said.

In the past, Catholics have met this psychological need for the feminine in God by attributing divine qualities to Mary. "But this creates even greater problems. It raises the question, 'Is Mary more merciful than God?' " Father Golden said.

According to Father Golden, the error we should attack is making God all male, a stern, unyielding Father. "We should attack this anthropomorphism. We have made God in the image of our distorted father," he said.

In his mind the question is not bringing femininity into God, for God is greater than femininity. God is boundless. If there is a problem with my original thesis, of seeing woman as an image of the Holy

54

Spirit, it is in falsely separating the traits of male and female. The real challenge for both men and women is the blending of traits society considers masculine and feminine.

A very real problem for men in the United States is their difficulty to show love. "The masculinity trap is a needless constriction on men," says Father Golden, referring to Myron Brenton's book, *The American Male.* "Men have been shoved into a trap," Golden said.

In *The American Male* Brenton lists characteristics considered masculine such as aggressiveness, stick-to-it-iveness, and reason, and those considered feminine: long-suffering, patience, co-operation. "This is a false classification. There should be masculine and feminine ways of expressing these qualities such as aggressiveness, initiative and patience," Father Golden said.

During our conversation Father Golden revealed his strong feelings about the male-female dichotomy. He really was deeply aggravated by the double standard. As a male, he resented the implication of the Traditional Nursery Rhyme: "Girls are sugar and spice and everything nice," while "Boys are sticks and snails and puppy dog tails."

"American men are cast in a false stereotype. They are cast in the impossible idea of John Wayne, on top of every situation. His word is never questioned. He never asks any questions," he said.

"This is hard to live up to," Father Golden said.

Some Notes from Father Golden about God

Since Rev. Thomas Golden holds a Ph.L. (Licentiate in Philosophy) from St. Lous University and was active in the campus ministry before coming to St. Francis, his background in philosophy and current psychological themes is extensive. He was an appropriate pastor for me to consult while interviewing for this book.

After reading my first draft, Father Golden wrote a little note which highlights some of the philosophical problems when writing of sex in God:

> *The problem is remembering when we speak of feminine or masculine in God that we are speaking anthropomorphically. God is not above sex, but He is beyond sex, i.e. transcends it.*
>
> *In the past some people have mistakenly attributed greater qualities of mercy to Mary than to God, for example, the* Little Cathechism *story that has Mary letting people who were refused by Peter and Jesus in through a trapdoor to heaven. Whatever mercy Mary has is because of the Father's mercy, not in spite of it.*
>
> *To give the impression Mary is more understanding than God is absolute heresy and should be shot down. Yet Mary's femininity and the high place of honor we give her is a remarkable vehicle of transmitting or manifesting God's mercy and love.*
>
> *The error is in our analogue of "male" which is just beginning to be freed from the stereotype of being stern, unyielding, adamant. We should enhance and enlarge this analogue by giving the ideal image qualities that should not be exclusively feminine: e.g. patience, understanding, adaptability.*
>
> *We forget St. Thomas's whole approach to predi-*

cating qualities that are in humans to God. We affirm the id quod *of the predication, but deny the* modus quo. *For example, some humans we know are loving, but God is All Loving, or God is Love as St. John says. The different qualities which seem to be at odds in man, e.g., mercy and justice, are one in God.*

Casting the Holy Spirit in the anthropomorphism of feminine will only lead us to the dangers of the distorted image that the Holy Spirit is a woman.

The Anima and Animus

In the early part of the twentieth century, Jung revolutionized Western thinking about the human person when he advanced the concept that a whole personality is comprised of masculine and feminine characteristics. Ultimately his work is affecting our imagery about God as we search for both masculine and feminine ways in which God operates within the totality of His Being.

According to Jung, neither a man nor a woman is a complete person unless he absorbs some basic traits considered characteristic of the opposite sex. Even further, Jung asserted that the psyche or soul for the male is feminine, *anima*, and for the female, masculine, *animus*.

It is in achieving a healthy relationship, a balance with this "other" within, that the person develops an integrated and whole personality. For the male, the "other" can be a witch, leading to hell, or ideal inspiration. Conversely, for the woman, the "other" can be dominant tyrant and lawgiver or liberating hero.

According to Jung, not just women, but men also are incomplete persons. This is revolutionary in Western psychology which has traditionally followed the thinking of Aristotle through Aquinas to Freud which viewed the woman as a mini or castrated male, somehow inferior. Woman has been described as the incomplete, passive force, and man as the active. The male has been considered the norm, the complete person.

In Jung's view it is not only the female who is half a person. So is the male.

Western culture has overlooked the importance of the feminine as a separate mode of being, according to Jung. He believed this to be devastating to the personality of the male who needs to open himself to love, to intuition, to non-rational modes of being in order to achieve wholeness. For the male to reach personality integrity, he must positively develop an accepted feminine characteristic, receptivity and surrender.

Outside the Jungian movement in psychology, totally apart from any behavioral science, the Christians in the Jesus movement have unconsciously recognized this need of the human person. They get at their *way* to personality wholeness through a little dramatic form, "To be born again you need to invite Christ into your heart as Lord."

"Jesus is the Way," they say.

Some of the earliest Christian mystics, like Origen, also recognized this feminine role of surrender, especially in the male Christian. They described this poetically, by calling the soul, even in the male, feminine. Allegorically, they viewed the soul of each

Christian, a bride of Christ.

Outside the mystical tradition, this surrender, identification with the "other," the Christ figure, has been more easily accomplished by the woman in our Western Christian culture. We readily accept and believe in Jesus Christ as Lord and Image of God, and we more readily accept this "surrender to the liberating Lord" imagery for the woman in our culture.

But it is difficult for both the male and female to move on from surrender to Christ to full psychological-religious maturity, to an integration of masculine and feminine, unless we can again identify with a feminine principle in God.

This needed imagery of the feminine prototype in God, is the much neglected role of the Holy Spirit or Hokmah or Sophia in Western civilization.

Six

WISDOM AND THE WORD:
"THE TWO HANDS OF GOD"

"I agree with you, there has to be the feminine in God," Dr. Joseph Blenkinsopp commented during an interview. Blenkinsopp had just read the second draft of my work and was explaining his criticisms of this premiminary effort.

He was obviously interested in the theme, the feminine in God. But as a scholar, he was quite critical of my original jump from the grammatically feminine *ruah* in Hebrew to the personification of the Spirit as *She*. "That weakens your argument," he said.

"I think you can build an argument on Wisdom and on personality," he advised, steering me to the sapiential or wisdom literature of the Old Testament.

During our conversation, Blenkinsopp indicated the Jewish writers or scribes did indeed write of Wisdom in feminine terms in their sapiential literature, especially in Proverbs, Wisdom, Sirach and Baruch. Although it is important to recognize that Wisdom and Sirach are not officially accepted by several Jewish and some Protestant sects, these books are all listed in the Roman Catholic Canon of the Bible.

Besides emphasizing the feminine personality of the Wisdom of God, Blenkinsopp further pointed out there is a suggestion of association between Wisdom and the Holy Spirit when Wisdom sings of Herself:

> *I came forth from the mouth of the Most High,*
> *and I covered the earth like mist.*
> *I had my tent in the heights, and my throne in a*
> *pillar of cloud (Ws. 24:3-6).*

Wisdom and Mary

While Joseph Blenkinsopp and I were discussing the need for a feminine imagery in God, the emphasis in our conversation shifted from the Holy Spirit and the feminine to Wisdom and the feminine, specifically to Mary. Briefly we touched on the identification of Mary with Wisdon on the liturgical level. I can remember insisting at one point during our discussion, "Popular liturgical Catholicism must be right, connecting Wisdom with Mary. There must be a relationship between Wisdom and Mary."

Blenkinsopp also thought this liturgical identification significant.

The liturgical association between Mary and the Wisdom tracts of the Old Testament is a spontaneous development in the history of the Church. According to Father Louis Bouyer, no specific Doctor of the Church or school of theology developed this concept. This association just happened in the Church, specifically in the popular liturgy of Eastern Christendom where the Wisdom texts were automatically applied to the Marian feasts.

The association between Wisdom and the feminine, either with Mary or the Holy Spirit, has always been a more popular concept in Eastern Christianity. The Catholic theologian, George Tavard, writes that this is especially true among the Russian Orthodox. In his book, *Woman in Christian Tradition*, in a chapter called "Orthodox Models," Tavard describes this attitude recorded graphically in Russian iconography:

> *... whereas the divine Sophia in the great Church of Byzantium is Christ, the Logos, several Russian Churches dedicated to Holy Sophia, like the cathedrals of Kiev and Novgorod, built in the eleventh century, extol a more feminine image of Sophia, embodied in the icon of the Virgin Mary.*

The Old Testament Wisdom, which is obviously a feminine personification, has been associated with Mary in both popular Catholicism and Eastern Christendom. This personification develops gradually in the sapiential literature, but in the New Testament She almost disappears except for one reference by Jesus. Luke records Jesus as speaking of Wisdom, continuing the feminine, motherly imagery: '... Yet, Wisdom has been proved right by all her children' (Lk. 7:35).

What happened to Wisdom in the New Testament? Is she identical with the Word as so many of the theologians have taught? Or is there another solution?

One possible answer for the disappearance of Wisdom is hinted at by the Scottish theologian James Wood in his work, *Wisdom Literature, an Introduction*. Using a metaphor, adaptable to the feminine imagery in the sapiential texts, Wood calls the Word, "Wisdom's fulfillment."

Another suggestion is that taught by three of the

earliest Fathers of the Church, St. Irenaeus of Lyons, Pope St. Clement of Rome, and Theophilus of Antioch. They identified Wisdom with the Holy Spirit who emerges as a new personification in the New Testament.

Whatever the theoretical discussion, the Gospels are dedicated to the Word of God, describing the Word made Flesh, just as earlier works revealed God's Wisdom. As the Word ascends in revelation history, Wisdom recedes into the background.

The question remains for Biblical scholars to determine, What did the prophetic writers mean by this feminine personification, Wisdom? Whatever the theoretical decision, popular Catholicism from its earliest days accommodated the Wisdom passages of the Old Testament to Mary, the Virgin Mother of God, *Theotokos.*

Wisdom and the Word: "The Two Hands of God"

The association of Mary with Wisdom indicates a split in thinking in the early Church between popular devotion and speculative thinking.

However, an almost forgotten metaphor of St. Irenaeus may help solve this speculative dilemma. Identifying the Holy Spirit with Wisdom, St. Irenaeus also called Wisdom and the Word, "the two hands of God."

Much of the theological speculation in our Western Christian tradition since the time of St. Justin has associated Wisdom with the Word. This tradition was originally initiated in the first century, B.C., by Philo of Alexandria, when he associated the Hebrew *Hokmah* or *Wisdom* with the Greek concept

64

of *Logos* or *Mind of God*. They were accommodating a Judaic-Christian revelation to a philosophic world steeped in the Platonic-Hellenic framework with its emphasis on Reason.

Many of the early scholars of the Church, continuing in the Hellenic rather than the Aramaic tradition, taught that St. Paul identified Wisdom with the Word when he called Christ, "wisdom of God" (1 Co. 1:30). However, it is interesting that this wisdom Paul writes of in this passage is not personified *Wisdom*, but appears more as a fruit of the Spirit. This is wisdom on the first level of Scripture as presented in the earliest Proverbs. This is a virtue, an attribute, not Wisdom personified.

Many scholars point to the close relationship between Solomon's claim for Wisdom in Ws. 9:9 as being "present" with Yahweh when He "made the world" and John's claim for the Word in Jn. 1:1:

In the Beginning was the Word:
The Word was with God
and the Word was God.

The section on "Wisdom" in *The Interpreter's Bible* lists many similar parallels between Wisdom in the Old Testament and the Word in the New Testament. They are both with God from the beginning: Wisdom "is a reflection of the eternal light, untarnished mirror of God's active power . . ." (Ws. 7:26), while the Word "is the radiant light of God's glory and the perfect copy of his nature . ." (Heb. 1:3).

There *is* a close relationship between Wisdom and the Word, but are they identical? Or is there a

65

slight difference between the two persons with Wisdom "a reflection of the eternal light" and a "mirror" of God's powers, while the Word is described as "the eternal light?" Only a slight difference in nuance, but it appears there is a subtle distinction between these two identities.

Even the uses of the nouns "reflection" and a "mirror" to describe Wisdom, add to this distinction. They are two more hints, suggestions, nuances of the essentially feminine quality of Wisdom.

"The Two Hands of God," St. Irenaeus's description of Wisdom and the Word, in my opinion, clarifies the relationship between these two Scriptural personalities. In this metaphor, Wisdom and the Word emerge, not as identical, but as similar, working together, as partners, to complete God's creation.

In *Wisdom Literature, an Introduction*, the Scottish theologian, Rev. James Wood, uses a similar metaphor, calling the very obvious similarities between Wisdom and the Word "a family resemblance."

Although Wood presents the traditional theology, he describes Jesus not as "Wisdom," but as a "wisdom teacher." According to Wood, Jesus was not a speculative philosopher in the Greek tradition. Jesus taught with wise sayings, proverbs, riddles, following in the tradition of the classical, Judaic Wisdom school. Developing on Wood's theme, Jesus was not Wisdom personified, but the fulfillment of the Judaic Wisdom tradition. Jesus was Wisdom's crowning achievement.

Several passages of Scripture indicate that Wisdom and the Word are not identical, but are closely related. They are inseparable, intertwined, at times almost synonymous as Jesus and the Spirit of Jesus are almost synonymous in the New Testament. As Wood explains, they indeed have a "family resemblance."

King David describes this double action of life within God as a union of *spirit* and *word* when he writes:

> *The spirit of Yahweh speaks through me, the word is on my tongue* (2 S. 23:2).

In Wisdom 9:1-2 it is not the *spirit of Yahweh* and the *word* working inseparably, but the *word* and the *wisdom* of God working hand in hand:

> *God of our ancestors, Lord of mercy, who by your word have made all things, and in your wisdom have fitted man . . .*

St. Irenaeus, disciple of St. Polycarp who in turn was a disciple of St. John the Evangelist, apparently grasped this Scriptural concept of the Word and Wisdom working together. He envisioned creation as a task of co-operation, similar to that outlined in 2 Samuel and the book of Wisdom. St. Irenaeus did not identify the Word with Wisdom as synonymous, but made them co-partners in creation. He named them together as the Word and Wisdom, Christ and the Spirit, calling them the "Two Hands of God."

Anyone who has paged through the *Encyclopedia Judaica Jerusalem* realizes the "Two Hands of God" is a common symbol on a Jewish "shivvite" or synagogue plaque. The two hands of God holding the

Torah, or scroll of the law, is a prominent metaphor in Jewish thought, a simile with Semitic overtones.

Besides being essentially Semitic, St. Irenaeus's imagery coincides more closely with my own concept of male and female as both in the image of God, co-partners with God in creation. With his description it is easier to make the intellectual leap from male and female in the image of God, to male and female in the image of the Word and Wisdom, Christ and the Holy Spirit.

St. Irenaeus's metaphor, "The Two Hands of God," allows for a theology of the feminine in God.

Seven

THE HELPER

(Jesus said):
"The Helper will come—the Spirit of truth, who comes from the Father. I will send him from the Father, and he will speak about me" (Jn. 15:26 Good News).

This direct naming of the Holy Spirit as *Helper* is very important, another clue to the archetypal feminine quality of the third Person in the Trinity. In Scripture, in Hebrew, the name reveals the essence. Jesus means *Savior.* That is what He *Is.* Paracletos means among other things, *Helper.* That is what the Spirit *Is.*

Significantly, *helper* is also the essence of woman, the name given to woman in Scripture. In various translations of Genesis 2:18 the woman is called: *companion, mate, helpmate, help, helper.*

No other English translation of the Greek, *Paracletos,* more graphically illustrates a link between the Holy Spirit and the feminine than the term *helper.* In my copies of the Bible, it is only the *Good News for Modern Man* translation which uses the word *Helper* to define the Holy Spirit. Other copies translate Paracletos variously as *advocate, paraclete, intercessor, friend.*

I first became aware of this use of the word, *Helper,* while reading John 14:25-26 in the *Good*

WOMAN, IMAGE OF THE HOLY SPIRIT

News for Modern Man:

> (*Jesus said*):
> '*I have told you this while I am still with you. The Helper, the Holy Spirit whom the Father will send in my name, will teach you everything, and make you remember all that I have told you.*'

The Helper, I thought while reading this passage. *That's exactly how woman is defined in Genesis.* It was a distinct moment of intuition for me. *The Spirit is Helper. The woman is helper. There is a relationship.*

Besides this direct naming of the Holy Spirit as Helper, many comparisons can be made in Scripture between the Holy Spirit and woman in the work they do. Genesis describes woman as partner and co-worker, while the Book of Proverbs in Chapter 31 shows this helper successfully working in a vast number of enterprises: managing a household, buying a vineyard, selling handmade goods at market, while the words of counsel are ever at her lips.

Wisdom, personified as the perfect housewife, is indeed a help, immensely practical.

The work of the Holy Spirit in Scripture has this same broad aspect. For the Spirit is intercessor, advocate, comforter, giver of life, creator of the new heart, is tower of flame, source of inspiration and wisdom. Most importantly, the Spirit is Helper.

Although the Spirit is defined as Helper in the New Testament, in the Old Testament this attribute or idea, Help, is incorporated into the essence of Yahweh. To be a Help is an aspect of the life of God.

70

The Helper

Yahwah describes Himself as Helper when the Spirit revealed through the prophet this attribute of His life:

Thus says Yahweh who made you, who formed you from the womb, who is your help (Is. 44:2).

St. Paul also understood helping as part of the life of God, when he wrote:

The Lord is my Helper, I will not be afraid (Heb. 13:6 NAB).

"A Fit Helper"

Yahweh God said, 'It is not good that the man should be alone. I will make him a helpmate' (Gn. 2:18).

Dr. J. Massingberg Ford and Dr. Edith Stein both examine the word, *helper*, in detail in their writings on woman. After studying the Hebrew in Gn. 2:18 they each concluded that this helper, or partner, has the connotation of something equal and complementary, really necessary to make a whole. Neither understand the Hebrew root for helper, *eser kenegdo* as signifying anything lesser or inferior. Dr. Stein was a leader in the Catholic woman's movement in Germany prior to World War II. She lectured extensively on the role of woman before entering, at the age of 42, the Carmelite convent in Cologne.

In one of her essys on woman, the *Vocation of Man and Woman According to Nature and to Grace*, Dr. Stein analyzes the meaning of the Hebrew *eser kenegdo* in Gn. 2:18. Explaining that the phrase is "almost untranslatable," she says it can mean "quite literally, that the woman is created as a help as it were quite opposite to man."

Vis-a-vis, the French term meaning *face-to-face*, is the expression used to capture the meaning of the Hebrew phrase, *eser kenegdo*, by the authors E. Danniel and B. Olivier in their book, *Woman is the Glory of Man*. *Vis-a-vis* would also have the connotation: counterpart, a mirror, a person created to help man discover himself. Scripture implies, therefore, that the woman is not a passive or inferior force, but the other half necessary for a mutually enriching dialogue.

The theologian J. Massingberd Ford uses the expression, *a helper fit for him*, in order to define the meaning of *eser kenegdo*. The concept, "fit helper," is essential to her conclusions on woman in her book, *The Spirit and the Human Person*. In her discussion of the subject Dr. Ford writes, "The Hebrew word contains the idea of similarity as well as supplementation and does not in any way seem to imply inferiority."

One idea Dr. Ford advances in her discussion of *eser kenegdo* is the concept that male alone is not the fullness of man. Rather, it is the male and female together that exemplifies the fullness of the Hebrew, *Adamah*, or mankind.

According to Dr. Ford, certain Jewish writers even consider the male somehow deficient in his humanity without the female in their interpretation of *eser kenegdo*. These Jewish writers, in the Kabbalistic tradition, believed it is woman who completes man, and that a male runs a real risk of being incomplete if he does not take a wife. Reflecting on Genesis 2:18, they reached the conclusion marriage affects the nature of the male. He is not really complete without the female.

Undoubtedly it is extreme to state that marriage is necessary for the male to achieve wholeness, as certain Jewish mystical sects still teach. This almost limits the male-female relationship to the physical, the sexual. But real face-to-face discourse, meaningful contact with women, is probably necessary for a man to achieve an integrated personality. *Eser Kenegdo* implies this.

For a balanced viewpoint, a male needs women friends, women co-workers, women associates in whatever his endeavor happens to be. Similarly women need male associates to develop integrated personalities.

Unfortunately, this *vis-a-vis* or counterpart relationship between a man and a woman is not always achieved in marriage. Here, too often, the relationship is out of balance, with either husband or wife striving for dominance. Or the relationship remains a mere sexual one, lacking a fully developed personal exchange.

Although the Jewish mystical writers of the Kabbalistic tradition might be extreme, they developed several centuries ago some themes which are emerging in modern psychology: the concept of the *animus* and the *anima*; the idea that men need to develop some feminine characteristics to achieve personality wholeness and vice versa, that women need to absorb some masculine qualities.

Today, child psychologists are telling us both parents are vital for balanced personality development of children. The boy needs to absorb some feminine qualities of tenderness, sympathy and love if he is to be fully human. On the other hand, the girl needs to take on the masculine qualities of courage, stability. Research in child development indicates that boys and girls normally achieve this healthy emotional balance in families where both father and mother are lovingly parenting.

Modern psychology indicates that parenting, mothering and fathering as it affects children, is a counterpart relationship. It is complementary, a mutually (and family) enriching dialogue, a *face-to-face* relationship.

"Wives, Fit in with Your Husband's Plans" (1 *P.* 3:1).

There is equality between male and female in marriage as between two counterparts. Yet the husband does have a special primacy in authority and the wife has a special primacy in love, according to the most recent papal teachings of the Church, and also according to Scripture.

This problem of the husband's authority arises, I believe, because we have a pagan concept of authority which is selfishly dominant, forcing subservience. This is not a Christian concept of authority. In a truly Christian home, authority is a role of service and liberation. In the Christian home authority does not fear "waiting on table" just as Jesus washed feet at the Last Supper and cooked his apostles a meal of fish after His Resurrection.

This question of authority in the home is best

74

solved, in my opinion, by the *Living Bible*'s translation of 1 P. 3:1: "Wives, fit in with your husband's plans." This translation comes closest to the role of wife outlined in Gn. 2:18 as that of "fit helper." This is a role of accommodation, a counterpart relationship, not subjection. The wife's role is "fitting in."

The *Living Bible* admonition to wives to "fit in with their husband's plans," adds to the dimension of Dr. Ford's "fit helper," to the French *vis-a-vis*, to Dr. Edith Stein's concept of mirror or counterpart. This does not delineate the role of wife or woman as one of being inferior, but rather of being adaptable.

Accommodation of self to the needs and desires of others, whether it be husband or child, is an accepted wifely-motherly virtue. It is also considered a feminine virtue, whether it be accommodating to the needs of patient, student or colleague.

In the home this adjusting, or compromising, is essential for peace and harmony. It is really a bending, not out of force or anger, but in love and joy, an adapting to the needs of others. In this flexibility harmony is created.

It is this kind of giving way in the home that summarizes this aspect of the feminine, to me, and perhaps summarizes an aspect of the unifying force within the Trinity. This is not a forced, but a willing yielding for wholeness, described with the imagery, "a fit helper."

Eight

SOME FEMININE IMAGERY ASSOCIATED WITH THE SPIRIT

The Paraclete: "By His Side"

> ... *when he laid down the foundations of the earth, I was by his side, a master craftsman, delighting him day after day (Pr.8:29b-30a).*

Throughout history various psychologies have defined woman as a passive force. Recently woman has been described more broadly as a passive-active force. The Paraclete can also be described as passive-active. Seen in this dimension of being both *passive and active, by the side of, sometimes silent*, the concept of Paraclete can take on a whole new connotation of meaning as the feminine aspect of God.

In Greek legal terminology a *paracletos* was someone who sat next to the accused, often not saying a word. He was a defense attorney, a spokesman, an intercessor. Sometimes he argued for the accused, but just as often he was standing by, just silent. The paracletos was called "louder than the loudest face."

The *Interpreter's Dictionary of the Bible* defines Paraclete as "one who stands to the side of." The word has a passive connotation of one who stands by to aid and succor, but there are also active extensions of the word. Thus, in the *Interpreter's Dictionary* the

Paraclete is also one "Who pleads as an 'advocate' (1 John 2:1) for someone, and so convinces and convicts, and also one who as a 'counselor' (KJV 'comforter'; John 14:16, 26; 15:26; 16:7) exhorts, strengthens, and comforts another."

If you examine these possible interpretations of *paracletos* outlined in the *Interpreter's Dictionary of the Bible* in a feminine, rather than a masculine perspective, then the work of the Holy Spirit becomes much more comprehensible. For then the Holy Spirit can be both advocate and life-giver and support, not as a lawyer defends his client but as a mother intercedes for her child.

If you view the Spirit as the intercessor for man with God, not as a lawyer in a court but as a loving Person, then you can begin to perceive an allegorical mother figure, as one who stands by the side.

In this sense of the mother figure being advocate for the father, his support and also an intercessor between father and child, the word *paraclete* fits in with all the other life-giving tasks of the Holy Spirit. These are the feminine tasks of giving spiritual birth, leading to truth, giving a new heart of love and joy to replace the old heathen heart of stone.

The notes in the *New American Bible* to the text, John 14, point out that *defense attorney* in the secular sense does not have the proper connotation for the context of John's Gospel. These notes say: "The Paraclete in John is a teacher, a witness to Jesus and a prosecutor of the world. He represents the continued presence on earth of the Jesus who has returned to the Father." The discussion on the meaning of the term, Paraclete, in the *New American Bible* allows for a possible interpretation of Paraclete as a feminine principle.

An even more significant connotation of Paraclete for my thesis is: *one who stands by the side of.* This is the very essence of Eve: from his rib, his side, the helper, counterpart, *vis-a-vis.* Eve is from the rib, the very side, the heart of man.

In the concept of the Greek Paracletos, we have the imagery "by his side" repeated in Scripture, linking the Paraclete figuratively to both Wisdom and to woman. In Genesis 2:21-22 woman is defined as being formed by Yahweh, from "the rib he had taken from the man."

Wisdom, the feminine personification associated with the Spirit in the Old Testament, is also one who stands by the side of Yahwah. In Pr. 8:29-30 Wisdom describes herself as ". . . by his side, a master craftsman, delighting him day after day. . . ."

In his book, *Wisdom Literature*, James Wood emphasizes this claim Wisdom makes for Herself, to be at the side of Yahweh, considering it very significant. Wood further points out that R.B.Y. Scott has suggested in *Vetus Testamentum* (April, 1960) this phrase "by the side of" can be translated, "Then I was at his side, a living link or vital bond."

Although Wood did not make the comparison between Eve, Wisdom and the Spirit, I did when reading his work. Wood was searching the meaning of Wisdom, but "by the side of as a living link or vital bond" meant Eve to me.

Later, when I discovered the definition of *paracletos* in the *Interpreter's Dictionary of the Bible* as "one who stands by the side of" I again made this intellectual leap to the feminine.

Added to this definition "by the side of" is the dimension of the Paraclete of being both passive and active, a support and an advocate combined. This is the classic definition of the feminine. Viewing the Paraclete as a prototype for feminine can help us understand the human principle of woman who is also both passive and active, receiving and giving, accepting and transforming.

Woman, like the Paraclete, is passive-active, is one who "stands by his side."

The Tower of Flame

Several years ago there was a popular song called, *Light My Fire*. Over and over again the artist sang, "Come on baby, light my fire, light my fire, light my fire." This song was quite vulgar, yet it illustrates what a young girl does to a young man in love. She knocks him over, wows him, sends him in a dizzy, sends his blood racing, makes him a new creature.

Is this passion something to be condemned? Or is it symbolic, if not perverted, of the intense love sparked in the person when the Holy Spirit touches the heart?

If the young girl sets the young man's heart aflame, so does the Holy Spirit. Our poetic religious literature is filled with the expression, "to set aflame." Prayers ask the Holy Spirit to enkindle our hearts with love for Jesus and the Trinity. Lives of the saints describe their mystical, ecstatic, almost passionate love affairs with God.

St. Therese of Lisieux, the Little Flower of

Jesus, describes in her *Autobiography* this experience of encountering God as a flame of fire. During an intense mystical moment in her life, she says she felt her heart was pierced with a burning sword of love. At this moment she felt enflamed with this love for God. The *Song of Songs*, which describes almost erotically the love affair between God and the soul, or Christ and the dove, calls this love of Yahweh:

> ... *a flash of fire, a flame of Yahweh himself. Love no flood can quench, no torrents drown* (Sg. 8:6b-7).

The Holy Spirit or presence of God often appears in the Old Testament as a Tower of Flame, just as It is described as wind or mist or breath of life. After the Exodus from Egypt, the Israelites were led through the desert for forty years by a cloud by day and a tower of flame by night. This tower of flame both strengthened and inspired this wandering Semitic tribe.

Again at Pentecost the Spirit came down upon Mary, the apostles and disciples as a roaring wind and tongues of fire. Rather than burn and consume those gathered in the upper chambers of that home in Jerusalem, the tongues of fire filled the apostles with courage. As if drunk with wine, they began babbling in new languages. They became men with hearts of courage, set aflame with the love of the Lord.

This is exactly what happens to a young man in love. He talks in a new language, sings songs of creation. He is given a heart of courage, is emboldened to deeds of valor. He is set aflame, not in the vulgar sense, but in a purified, rarified way. He is given a

WOMAN, IMAGE OF THE HOLY SPIRIT

new heart of love, just as the Holy Spirit creates the
new heart as St. Paul describes in Rm. 5:5:

*... because the love of God has been poured into our
hearts by the Holy Spirit which has been given us.*

Flame can be both destructive and the source of
power and light, just as the flame of human love can
either destroy, or foster extra-ordinary creativity.
Atomic energy is an example of this. The flames released through atomic energy could conceivably set
off a holocaust. But if controlled, if released rational-
ly, this energy stored in the atom is powerful enough
to eliminate pollution and light up the whole world.
    Flame destroys. It also enlightens and purifies.
The Bible is resplendent with the imagery of fire pur-
ifying the soul: Is. 1:24; Zc. 13:9; Ml. 3:2-3; Si. 2:5.
Jesus describes the beginning of this purification in
Luke 12:49 when He says, "I have come to bring fire
to the earth and how I wish it were blazing already."
    John the Baptist predicts this purification of
love which will be wrought through Jesus and His
Spirit when he says in Matthew 3:11:

*I baptize you in water for repentance, but the one who
follows me is more powerful than I am, and I am not fit
to carry his sandals; he will baptize you with the Holy
Spirit and fire.*

The Spirit Led Jesus Into the Desert
    The fire of the Holy Spirit purifies, enflames the
heart with love for Jesus, but it also enlightens.
Throughout Scripture the work of the Holy Spirit is

82

to inspire and to lead. In the Old Testament the spirit of Wisdom, like a cloud by day and a tower of flame by night, led the Israelites through the Sinai Peninsula on to the Promised Land. The Prophets, too, were inspired by the Spirit to praise God in psalm and song.

In the New Testament the Spirit is still leading, first Jesus and later the Church. As one commentator about the Holy Spirit says, "In Luke the Spirit leads Christ. In Acts the Spirit leads the Church."

One of Jesus's first public acts is recorded in the Gospels after He was baptized by John the Baptist. Luke reports that after Jesus was filled with the Holy Spirit:

> *Jesus left the Jordan and was led by the Spirit through the wilderness, being tempted there by the devil for 40 days (Lk. 4:1).*

Leading, beckoning onward is the work of the Holy Spirit in Scriptures as the Evangelist writes in Jn. 16:13, "when the Spirit of truth comes he will lead you to the complete truth. . . ."

In this leading a person, beckoning him onward, woman is very much like the Holy Spirit. Perhaps there is no other section of Scripture that reveals this very essential side of woman more clearly than the story in the Garden of Eden. Here, Eve encourages Adam to eat of the forbidden fruit, of the tree of the knowledge of good and evil, to forget the Creator and become like a god. Eve leads Adam astray.

The story in the garden illustrates the very essence of fallen woman: to lead astray, to seduce, to lure a man away from the commandments of the Father. This is the role of Dame Folly, described in Proverbs 9:13-15, 17: acting on impulse, childish and knowing nothing, inviting the passers-by, whispering seductively, "Stolen waters are sweet." Ancient mythology recognizes this very destructive side of woman, portraying it as a demonic force.

In contrast, the good woman leads a man to visions, beckons him to the Father. Like the Holy Spirit in Scripture, woman in the fullness of her goodness is an inspiration to man. Historically, one woman after another has inspired men to great deeds. Joan of Arc led a weak and struggling French army to its full manhood, able to fight off the English conqueror. Dante had his Beatrice, Shakespeare his Lady. The Knight of the Middle Ages also fought for his Lady, his shining light, the paragon of virtue.

History also continuously records the feminine as luring to disaster: Helen of Troy, Cleopatra, Delilah.

It seems there is a parallel of opposites between the story of Eve luring Adam to be tempted in the Garden of Eden and the tale of the Spirit leading Christ into the desert to be tempted. During the first temptation scene Adam fell, was expelled from the garden. In the second temptation story, Christ was not led into a garden. Just the opposite. He was led by the Spirit into the desert, into a land of desolation, there, not to succumb, but to overcome temptation.

In the desert, history was reversed.

Do these two accounts of temptation illustrate a psychological truth, the two sides of feminine nature?

Some Feminine Imagery Associated with the Spirit

Is there a parallel between these two beckoning
forces? One fallen? The other "the purest emanation
of the breath of God?"

I believe there is a parallel. In the garden story
Eve is enticing Adam to disaster. In the Gospel ac-
count it is the Spirit of God who is leading Christ, the
New Adam, to victory.

Nine

"THE RIB OF THE LOGOS"

How does a substance proceed, but not by generation? This has been a thorny question debated by theologians about the Holy Spirit throughout Church history.

In the fourth century St. Gregory of Nazianzus, one of the Cappadocian Fathers in Asia Minor, pointed to a way out of this theological dilemma about the processions within the Trinity, during one of the Church conflicts. He suggested that Eve proceeded from the rib of Adam, not by generation.

Gregory of Nazianzus asked if Eve's mysterious creation from the rib of Adam is a possible analogy in nature to the means of procession in the Trinity.

Earlier another Eastern bishop, St. Methodius of Olympus, specifically described the Holy Spirit as the "costa Verbi," that is the "rib of the Logos."

A poet and mystic rather than a theologian, this third century bishop and martyr stressed the archetypal relationship between Adam and Christ. He called Adam the first man, born of the virgin earth, and Christ the archvirgin, born of a virgin mother. In poetic flights he described the rise of the soul to God, the mystical sleep of Christ giving birth to the Church—the New Eve, and the marriage of Christ and the Virgin Church.

Throughout his writings St. Methodius of Olympus stressed purity as an essential virtue for this union with Christ which was the work of the Holy Spirit. This is the One he described as "the rib of the Logos."

Late in the nineteenth century Matthias Joseph Scheeben revived the thinking of St. Gregory of Nazianzus and St. Methodius of Olympus in his great work, *The Mysteries of Christianity*. More of a mystical theologian than a speculative one, Scheeben explains his attraction to mystery in the first chapter of his book. He states that the reduction of Christianity to a "rational science" betrays Christianity which "is a mystery." Mystics like St. Methodius appeal to Father Scheeben.

In an appendix to this book, Scheeben uses St. Gregory's analogy between the creation of Eve and the procession of the Holy Spirit and St. Methodius' description of the Spirit as the "rib of the Logos" in an attempt to explain how the Spirit proceeds from the Word. He describes St. Gregory of Nazianzus' analogy between Eve and Adam's rib, the Spirit and the side of Christ, as "brilliantly illustrating the doctrine of the Trinity."

Although he was careful to state this is only a comparison, Father Scheeben thought the Spirit might proceed from the side of Christ on the Cross in a similar manner to Eve's procession from the rib of Adam. Scheeben writes, "And as Eve can, in a figurative sense, be called simply the rib of Adam, since she was formed from the rib of Adam, St. Methodius goes so far as to assert that the Holy Spirit is the *costa Verbi*. . . ."

The Growing Acceptance of the Concept

Father Scheeben's revival of two of the Greek Fathers' analogies between the Holy Spirit and the feminine, in my opinion helps solve the problem of definition, both of woman and of the Spirit. These metaphors get at the essence of the Trinity, unity of Persons in the same Nature. And they also capture the essence of humanity, unity and equality of male and female in the same nature. They open the door to a theology of the feminine in God.

Nineteenth and twentieth century theologians like Father Scheeben are giving us a needed new breadth of concept of Holy Spirit and analogously to our idea, woman. They are beginning to see a link between the two, asking if there is a relationship.

It is only now in the late nineteenth and twentieth centuries that this idea of affinity between Spirit of God and the feminine is becoming more acceptable in the Western Christian tradition, which has been based on a more speculative Hellenism. The idea of a necessary feminine principle within the Trinity appears to be gaining approval as C. G. Jung has revolutionized Western psychology and as Western theologians turn to Eastern Christianity for new insights.

George A. Tavard, in his book *Woman in Christian Tradition*, writes of several Russian Orthodox theologians of the late nineteenth and early twentieth centuries who attempted to discover the feminine element in God. These include Vladimir Soloviev, Sergius Bulgakov and Paul Evdokimov, all of whom see a relationship between the feminine and either the

Spirit or Wisdom. Tavard says of these men: "It is in Russian theology that the question of the female aspect of God has been raised directly."

Although Father Tavard apparently questions some of the conclusions contained in Russian sophiology, he writes, "The exact whereabouts of the divine archetype of the feminine remains a moot question, one which may well forever escape analysis. Yet it would seem femininity must somehow be related to the Spirit."

Many Christians and Jews, especially those in the Aramaic tradition, have always believed that the Holy Spirit or Wisdom or the Hebraic Shekhinah represented the feminine prototype in the Trinity or in the Deity. Among the Kabbalistic Jews, who stress a Judaism of the heart, certain mystical writers describe the Shekhinah, the Presence of God, as the feminine aspect of the God-head.

The idea of the Spirit as feminine also appears among the Syriac Fathers in whose language *spirit* and *air* were feminine. It also occurred among some of the Aramaic Gnostic sects of early Christianity. It has been hinted at by a few of the Fathers of the Church, generally among those in a more mystical or Semitic tradition.

One of these, the fourth century poet St. Ephrem of Syria, describes the "breath of air" or Spirit as "a mother nursing with her entire body." In Hymn XI St. Ephrem described this air of Paradise as "the delightful source which Adam sucked when he was young. Like a breast, this air nourished his childhood."

According to Father Tavard, who writes of St.

Ephrem, "In the Syriac language used by Ephrem the word 'air' is feminine, which renders the image plausible." Describing the comparison St. Ephrem makes between the Spirit and mothering in his book, *Woman in Christian Tradition*, Tavard says, "The poems of Ephrem of Syria present the interesting characteristic that they are purely Semitic and totally innocent of Hellenism."

"Spirit of Spirit"

In *Woman is the Glory of Man* the authors, E. Danniel and B. Olivier, document the growth of the idea, woman is in the image of God. In this volume the authors cite several writers of the late nineteenth and early twentieth centuries who have proposed this idea, including Linus Bopp, Louis Bouyer and Edith Stein. Edith Stein asks this essential question about woman as made in the image of God. In an article, "The Problems of Women's Education," she writes:

> *We may ask whether this womanhood that is serving love is a real image of the Godhead. Serving love means assistance that helps all creatures to lead them to perfection. Now this is the title that is given to the Holy Ghost. Thus we could see the primeval type of feminine being in the Spirit of God that is shed abroad over all creation.*

In her writings on woman, Edith Stein synthesizes several trends of thought. She was a Jewish scholar with a solid background in Hebrew, a Jewess brought up in a devout household. She was also a phenomenologist with an international reputation in pre-Nazi Germany. After her conversion to Catholocism she attempted to co-ordinate these many trends with Scripture and the tradition in the Church, especially Scholasticism.

As a philosopher Dr. Stein believed that all created being reflected the Supreme Being. As a woman, she realized she was different from the male. Writing in the Scholastic tradition, she thought woman has to be different, because her form is different. She also knew in her soul, as a deeply prayerful person and from her meditations on Scripture, she was made in the image of God.

Stein re-inforced my notion that woman is made in the image of God, specifically the Spirit of God.

Matthias Joseph Scheeben added to it, calling the Spirit, after the metaphor of St. Methodius, "the rib of the Logos." This was a whole new poetic image for me. So were all Scheeben's concepts of procession and spiralling, twin actions of knowing and loving that I gleaned, poring through his treatise on the Trinity.

As poetic truth, Scheeben's thought, the rib of the Logos, helped crystalize both the mystery of the Trinity and the mystery of the Spirit for me. Just as Adam went into a deep sleep and Eve was formed by Yahweh, not by generation but by a mysterious procession from Adam's rib or side, so the Spirit proceeded from the rib of Christ pierced with a lance on Calvary. This is a beautiful analogy.

Scheeben explains the thought further. *Woman* describes the nature of the feminine as part of humanity. She is from man, from Adamah, who is *from the earth*. This same principle in the Godhead cannot be called woman, because It is not from the earth. No, the name for this same principle in God is Spirit, because God is spirit.

In *The Mysteries of Christianity* Scheeben writes:

> *If Eve was called "woman" because she was taken from "man," the Third Person in God must be named after the persons from whom He proceeds. He must be called Spirit, because He proceeds from the Father and the Son inasmuch as both are one Spirit: He is Spirit of Spirit.*

The Fountain of Living Water

The Spirit of God proceeds from both the Father and the Son, according to Church dogma. Scripture upholds this apparent contradition. For the spirit of God was with the Father from the very beginning in Genesis when the earth was a formless void and God's spirit hovered over the water.

Scripture indicates that the Spirit is sent by both the Father and the Son. In John 14:26 Jesus describes this mysterious action: ". . . but the Advocate (or Helper), the Holy Spirit whom the Father will send in my name, will teach you everything and remind you of all that I have said to you."

After the death of Christ, this same Spirit proceeds from the Son, from his side in blood and water upon Calvary when Christ "bowing his head . . . gave up his spirit" (Jn. 19:30).

There is a kind of irrational contradiction about the Spirit in Scripture. For this Spirit of God was with God from the very beginning of time, searching the mind of God (Wisdom). This same Spirit proceeding from the Father could move across the earth, quickening all life, inspiring prophets, leading a band of wandering nomads across desert and mountain (Wisdom), touching the psalmist with ode and song.

The very same Spirit proceeding from the Father could hover over Mary, overshadowing her (as a cloud, as the Presence of God), so that the seed of the woman (Gn. 3:15) could flower into the Son of Man. Through the will of the Father the Spirit hovered over Mary and the Son of God became flesh.

On the Cross, the Spirit proceeded again, as it were, from the Rib of the Logos, from the breast of Christ. The Spirit proceeded from the bosom of Christ, according to Scheeben, at the thrust of a lance, in blood and water.

After the Ascension of Christ the Spirit proceeded again, this time to descend at Pentecost hovering over the earth in a new way. In this new role, the Holy Spirit began re-forming each new Christian, born again of water and the Spirit, into a child of God, another Christ.

Is this one and the same Holy Spirit, first proceeding from the Father to quicken all life; then working hand in hand with the Word to form all creation; then hovering over Mary to transform the Word into flesh; and then proceeding again through Christ, building up the Bride of Christ, His Church?

The Fathers of the Church teach this is one and the same Spirit, proceeding in some mysterious way from both the Father and the Son, bestowing life in an ever-widening circle, spirating endlessly as Dom David Steindl-Rast describes it, as the "endless babble of creation."

This Holy Spirit is an ever-onrushing river of life, the fountain of living water proceeding from the breast, the side, the rib of Christ. As Scripture declares:

From his breast shall flow fountains of living water (Jn. 7:38).

Ten

TO KNOW AND TO LOVE:
THE TRINITY IN EACH OF US

Theologians teach us Knowing and Loving is the double action or twin action of the God-life, personified in the second and third Persons of the Trinity, the Word and the Spirit.

This twin action is reflected in each individual soul: knowing and loving, or knowing and willing. It is further represented graphically as an external expression of the human race: in man, the embodiment of knowing, and in woman, the embodiment of love.

Because the human race is divided into male and female, however, does not mean there should be a split within each person, either all male and knowing, or all female and loving. To the contrary, the androgynous male-female personality is the Christian ideal. The end for each Christian is to mirror the whole Trinity.

There is a Trinity in each of us.

Male and Female: To Know and to Love
The French theologian Antonin Marcel Henry, O.P., writes in *The Holy Spirit* that God's life is an "eternal act of knowledge and love" and that this image of God shows forth in us when we know and love God.

Although the theologians Karl Rahner and

97

Matthias Joseph Scheeben both repeat this theological speculation about the Trinity, they also look beyond theology to an analogy in nature. Scheeben sees an analogy between the emergence of Eve from Adam's rib and the Spirit flowing from the breast of Christ on the Cross. In *The Trinity* Rahner cries out against the cold, theological formulas, with no apparent relationship to life.

"Nature must express the Trinity," he insists.

Rahner finds it hard to relate much of the Church's accumulation of theological disputations on the Trinity with his concept of an experiential, personal God. He finds it even more difficult to make any connection between the theological concepts of the Trinity and the doctrine of creation. In his discussion he exclaims, "The isolation of the treatise of the Trinity *has* to be wrong. There *must* be a connection between the Trinity and man."

Looking at mankind, we can observe that Rahner is right. There is a noticeable relationship between the Trinity and man. The double-action life of the Trinity of knowing and loving is everywhere expressed in humanity as male and female. Though man and woman are of one human nature, they do reflect this double mission of God, to know and to love. There is an analogy between Logos and Agape, male and female, Word and Spirit.

In most cultures the male is accepted as the symbol of rational knowledge, knowledge of the head. Man is the builder, the creator of cities. He governs, dams rivers, shapes airplanes, plans flights to the moon, splits atoms, searches the stars. He is knowledge externalized, exemplifying the Word made

Flesh.

Then there is woman, not a mini male as so many philosophers have falsely assumed, but an entity in herself, a different aspect of humanity, a being far more interior, even more inclined to the mystic. As Edith Stein, reflecting her Scholastic background says, "Woman's form is different, so her soul must be different." (Thinking of *soul* as C. G. Jung does, as feminine in the male and masculine in the female, allows for a difference in the woman's soul without making her inferior. Equal, but different, is a more accurate term.)

Woman, as such, is not generally the builder of things—although there are many notable exceptions. Rather, the feminine nurtures, protects, accommodates herself to the needs of others. She nurses, heals, teaches, guides, consoles, inspires. She is more concerned with inner space, the inside of houses, of schools, of hospitals. Her life is inner directed. She is inclined to the interior.

Man is symbolized by the Appolonian reason, the building of things, by external action.

Woman is symbolized by wisdom of the heart, by Sophia, by transforming souls, by the moon ever reflecting the light of the sun. Throughout history, woman has been identified with that universal symbol of love, the dove.

This analogy seems apparent to me. But evidently it has not been obvious to the theologians reared in the Western Christian tradition who have consistently denied that the feminine as such is in the image of God. To Western theological Christianity, woman has remained a mystery, hidden literally and figuratively behind the veil.

Philosophers of the Western Church, until the recent century, have not undertaken the task of understanding woman.

Perhaps this is the reason the Trinity has remained veiled in a shroud of mystery.

In Christ, Unity:

> ... *there are no more distinctions between Jew and Greek, slave and free. male and female, but all of you are one in Christ Jesus (Ga. 3:28).*

According to C. G. Jung, sexual differences are basic, reflecting inherent structural polarities of the human personality. They are not biological accidents, but reflect something essential in the human person. Jung asserted that for the male this inner psyche is feminine, and for the female, masculine. He recognized a polarity, a twinness, in each human being.

Jung also taught that the healthy personality would achieve a balance with "the other" within, would be a blend of masculine and feminine characteristics. In the male, however, it is likely the masculine characteristics will still predominate, and in the female, the feminine would still probably be dominant.

If Jung is right, does his concept of polarity in each individual reflect the essential twinness in God, revealed in the Trinity? Does Jung's *animus* and *anima* in some way mirror the twin action of the Deity, Word and Love? Does the human race manifest itself as an expression of God as male and female, reflecting the eternal actions of Word and Love?

Does each individual soul? Are we each an expression of Word and Love, as Jung explains, a healthy balance between masculine and feminine? Are we each an expression of Trinity?

I would say, *Yes, we are.*

The goal for each person, especially the Christian is psychic wholeness, a mirroring of Trinity. Integrity of the human person demands a balance of masculine and feminine characteristics: logic with intuition, knowledge of the head with wisdom of the heart. Each of us reflect, not just one Person in God, but the whole Trinity.

The early Fathers of the Church recognized this personality wholeness often achieved by the Christian. They wrote of the "soul" as feminine, many such as Origen describing the soul as "the bride of Christ."

The Fathers also were aware that through Christianity women apparently overcame the subservient and inferior condition of their sex in the predominantly pagan culture. During the Patristic Period both Ambrose and Jerome observed that by believing in Christ a woman would cease to be a woman and would become male.

Although these Fathers of the Church were not speaking in modern psychological terms, they did perceive the balancing of masculine-feminine characteristics achieved in the Christian process. The Christian mystic, although male, became feminine in his soul in his relation to Yahweh, while the Christian woman was raised above her cultural level of inferiority to masculine scholarship and equality of intellect.

This blend of masculine-feminine characteristics is not only observable in mature Christians. The androgynous personality is also characteristic of the Persons of God.

Jesus, the obvious male personification in the Trinity, displays many markedly feminine characteristics. He was patient, suffered the little children, displays the many fruits of the Holy Spirit that culture ascribes to the feminine: long-suffering, wisdom, understanding, counsel, piety.

Dame Julian of Norwich, the twelfth century English recluse, was particularly aware of the obvious blend of masculine-feminine characteristics in the person of Jesus Christ. Conscious of the needed motherhood in God, comparing Jesus to the Wisdom of the Old Testament, she called Jesus, "our very Mother."

Similarly, the Holy Spirit, who is the more feminine personification in the Trinity, displays a blend of feminine-masculine characteristics. Although described as the source of spiritual birth in Scripture, the Holy Spirit is also described by St. Paul as ruler, as Lord:

Now this Lord is the Spirit, and where the Spirit of the Lord is, there is freedom (2 Co. 3:18).

The Trinity Within

Karl Rahner writes in *The Trinity* that each of the three persons in God communicates Himself to man "in his own particularity and diversity." God does not reveal Himself to man only as the Father or Source or unoriginate, but He also expresses Himself in all three modes of His subsistence, as Father, Son

102

and Spirit.

Rahner's explanation conforms to my own experience of God, for I do experience God in three different ways. I have a sense of God as *up there*, the Father, a primordial substance above and beyond. But I also experience God *within*, inside me (the Spirit) and as brother *beside me* (Christ). I do experience God as three distinct realities: transcendent, immanent in myself and as an external expression.

The ego that is my consciousness does feel this God in three distinct manners: as God the Father in the Heavens; as God the Christ, my Brother and Sister in all things; and as God, the Life-giving force within me, the Spirit.

There is a Trinity in each of us, a sense of the Ultimate Being and a capacity to know and to Love that Source. We recognize in our soul three different relationships to God: an acceptance or intuition of a primordial Being; the thrust to know and understand that Being; and an emotion, sometimes a passion, to love. Many philosophers, theologians and psychologists have approached this Trinity within in a variety of ways. They recognize in some way these distinctions: a mindless sensing of the Deity, and a knowing, then a loving of this Person.

Carl Jung in his psychological studies recognized this something within as "the other," calling it *animus* in the female, *anima* in the male. St. Augustine described a Trinity in our nature, relating our *memory* to the Father, the *understanding* to the Son and our *will* to the Spirit.

St. Paul states this simply in 1 Th. 5:23 that man is made up of "spirit, soul and body."

As we grow in our relationship to God, we sense more and more there is a Trinity operating within us. As we relax our being, letting ourselves fall into the hands of the Father, just yielding our soul, we begin to sense the Ultimate Being. And we become aware of our capacity both to know and to love that Source. We become healed. We become whole.

Eleven

THE MIXED METAPHOR OF THE SPIRIT: MARY AND THE DOVE

There is such a breadth of imagery associated with the Holy Spirit in Scripture. This mixed metaphor is breathtaking: the spirit of God, Wisdom, somehow associated with the flowering of the seed of the woman and with Mary, overshadowing, ever with overtones of the feminine.

Yet, this imagery of the Spirit of God is always closely related to both the Father and the Word—the Holy Mist, the Presence of God, the Cloud which the Son of Man will ride from heaven in the last days as a throne. The Spirit, the Cloud, the Shekhinah, the Glory of God, the Heavenly Mist or Breath, the Son of Man riding the Wind: it is a poetry of God.

Perhaps this is where we have erred in our discussions on the Spirit, trying to box this unfathomable Person into a theological, rational treatise. For the Spirit is not a syllogism. The Spirit is Wisdom, a Tower of Flame, a Tongue of Fire, a Cloud leading a wandering nomadic tribe of itinerant Israelites.

The Spirit is Poetry.

The Holy Spirit is also the action of God making His Word concrete, inspiring the Word into the mind of the prophet, enfleshing the Idea in matter. The Latin expresses vividly this concept, the *mater* or *mother* forming the human spirit or soul into matter.

Mater, the root for *material* or *matter*, contains the notion, idea materialized: the Word made Flesh.

The Spirit is the Breath of God, the Wind, inspiration, guiding the craftsman who is "wise of hand." The Spirit was with God from the beginning, is described in Wisdom as "consort" of Yahweh's throne and in the Gospels appears in the symbol of the Dove.

What is the Meaning of the Dove?

What is the meaning of this Dove? How have we overlooked this metaphor so closely linked with the Holy Spirit in the New Testament and in Genesis? We in the Western world have ignored this allegory. Yet there it is in Scripture, boldly proclaiming a mystical link between the spirit of God and the feminine. For in the ancient world the dove is associated with the feminine, is an age-old symbol of love.

According to the *Encyclopedia Judaica Jerusalem* the dove is a symbol of love, beauty and innocence in the ancient Judaic world. This Dove often symbolizes the Holy Spirit in Scripture.

The Spirit appears as a Dove, bringing the olive branch of renewal to Noah and mankind, hovering over the Son of Man in the Jordan, like the mist that first hovered over the waters of Genesis.

Dove, water, new life . . .

The dove also represents the heavenly bride, the soul, the spouse of Christ, the New Jerusalem, in both Zepheniah and the Song of Songs. In the Douay version of Zepheniah (Sophonias), Chapter 3:1, Jerusalem is described as "the provoking and redeemed city, the dove."

106

The dove, as beloved, also appears in the great love poem in Scripture, the Song of Songs. In *The Struggle with God*, the Russian Orthodox theologian Paul Evdokimov writes, "The Canticle of Canticles sings the espousals of the Word and the dove."

In the Canticles or Song of Songs the "dove" is considered to be another name for the bride, the spouse of Christ, the soul, the New Jerusalem. In this rhapsodic love poem, celebrating the love of Christ for the soul, the Bridegroom, or Christ, is calling:

Open to me, my sister, my love, my dove, my perfect one (Sg. 5:2b).

Is this impossible, conflicting imagery? Is there a contradiction between the image of the dove in the Song of Songs and the emergence in the Gospels of the Dove hovering over the Son of God being baptized in the Jordan?

Or is this complementary imagery? Does the dove symbolism tell us something about the quality of the love relationship between Yahweh and the soul? Does it tell us something about the love relationship within the life of the Trinity? For the dove is the ancient symbolism of both beauty and innocence.

Somehow, in a manner beyond our human understanding, the Spirit appears in various sections of Scripture to fulfill all three roles of the feminine: mother, sister and bride. Similarly, the dove is related to different aspects of the feminine.

The Spirit, as wisdom, is presented as "consort," working by the side of Yahweh (Pr. 8:29). Then the Spirit appears almost as the primeval God-Mother in

Mt. 1:18, where the Word is made Flesh "by the power of the Spirit." Later, in a manner similar to a New Eve, the Spirit of God, is an ever-flowing fountain of living water proceeding from the breast of the Son (Jn. 7:38).

From a human viewpoint, this seems impossible. But this is not human, it is on the God level. It is a life in the spirit, for God is Spirit. It is as Spirit, "the pure emanation" (Ws. 7:25), that the Holy Spirit lives out the Song of Songs imagery of the Dove.

Mary: "A Very Special Likeness to the Spirit"

Anyone who has stood in wonder at the foot of the image of Our Lady of Guadalupe in the famous shrine in Mexico City knows there is something special about Mary. In some unfathomable way she represents the woman of Revelations 12:1: "adorned with the sun, standing on the moon." Mary is image of the eternal feminine. Yet Mary is not God.

In some manner Mary is related to all the feminine imagery associated with the Holy Spirit: Tent of Yahweh, Seat of Wisdom, Glory of God.

The Second Vatican Council recognized this symbolic relationship between Mary and the Holy Spirit, perhaps unconsciously, calling Mary, *Advocate, Helper*. The Council affirmed these titles, previously granted by the Church, describing Mary with names of the Holy Spirit in Scripture.

The Church has also spontaneously in its popular liturgy identified Mary with the Wisdom passages of the Old Testament. This is the same Wisdom the earliest Fathers of the Church identified with the Spirit of God.

The Mixed Metaphor of the Spirit: Mary and the Dove

Since the Virgin Mary is often associated with Holy Sophia in Russian iconography, it is not surprising to find her identified with the Holy Spirit by the Russian Orthodox scholar, Sergius Bulgakov. In *Le Paraclet* or *The Holy Spirit*, Bulgakov states: "Man is created in the image of God, but this image is precisely the Theanthropy, the image of the Father. The image of the Father is the Son, revealed in the Godman, and the Holy Spirit, revealed in the Mother of God."

In the *Wisdom of God* Bulgakov again compares the Virgin Mary, the Mother of God, to the Spirit. "She is, in personal form, the human likeness of the Holy Ghost," he says.

According to the French Catholic theologian, Father Louis Bouyer, there is a relationship between the Holy Spirit and Mary. But not as spouse and bride, he insists in his book, *The Seat of Wisdom*. A hint of a sexual relationship between the Spirit and Mary is unthinkable, according to Bouyer. Sex can not be in God, not like the mythological fables.

Rather, Mary takes on many of the qualities describing the spirit of Yahweh in the Old Testament, Bouyer observes. She becomes tent of Yahweh, literally the House of God, then mother of the Church, protector of the New Jerusalem.

Father Louis Bouyer sees the relationship between the Holy Spirit and Mary as a poetic, symbolic one. He describes the Spirit hovering over Mary as Tent, as Presence, as Cloud overshadowing, reaching out to Mary by way of assimilation, reaching out to Mary for personification. In Mary, Father Louis Bouyer sees, "a very special likeness to the Spirit."

109

Twelve

"THERE IS A SEASON ..."

Every idea has its Time.

There was a Time in Salvation History when the prophets developed the concept of Yahweh, the Father, and another era which focused on the divinity of the Logos, the Word made Flesh. This International Woman's Year, 1975, symbolized by the Dove, appears to be the time for a growing awareness of the Holy Spirit.

It is the year of the feminine principle in God.

It is significant that the concepts of the Holy Spirit as allegorically feminine, or as feminine principle in the Deity, are not totally alien to Christianity. Mystical and poetic writings describing the Holy Spirit with feminine imagery can be found sporadically among the earliest Fathers and through the twenty-century evolution of Christianity.

The seeds of this idea have long been lying dormant in the Church, waiting to be fully developed. This is not a new process, for other doctrines, such as the Assumption and the Trinity, have gradually grown and been defined. Growth of doctrine characterizes our Judaic-Christian heritage.

In *Woman in Christian Tradition*, in his chapter "Orthodox Models," Tavard comments, ". . . enough ingredients were available in the theology of the Greek Fathers to open the way to a theology of the

111

feminine in God." In this chapter he observes that recent Russian Orthodox theologians have pioneered in developing a *sophiology* which Tavard defines as: *a systematic attempt to discover the feminine element in God and to understand it in terms that are compatible with traditional Trinitarian faith.*

A Tradition of the Semitic School

The image of the Holy Spirit as feminine or as described with feminine poetic imagery or as somehow related to the feminine is a tradition which appears most often in branches of Christianity which are still Semitic in thought. It appears among Eastern sects of Christianity, especially among the Syriac, Aramaic and Orthodox Fathers. It also appears in Jewish mysticism where the spirit of God or Shekhinah was thought of as feminine.

The idea was suggested or hinted at by several of the early Greek Fathers of the Church and appears as a thread in the poetical writings and liturgical prayers of the Church. The poets of the Church have consistently used feminine imagery to describe the actions of the Holy Spirit.

But the concept has never been officially accepted in the theology of the Western Church, based on Hellenic tradition in Greek thought. The psychology and theology that developed in this western framework were essentially Hellenic rather than Semitic. It was Appolonian, stressing the knowledge of the head, the Greek concept of Logos or Mind of God. The Word or Idea, unhindered by matter or the flesh, is one aspect of this Greek thinking. Pure reason, the masculine unaffected by the feminine, was the supreme spiritual principle.

Since the Alexandrian school thought of woman as inferior and passive, it followed logically that the female as such could not be in the image of God. How could a person that was inferior contain the full image of the Divinity? The only solution for many of the Fathers, was that through Christianity, the female became male.

In contrast, the Semitic tradition (as expressed in Genesis and Proverbs, although not in some rabbinic or Talmudic practices) did not treat woman as inferior. On the contrary, as originally defined in the Old Testament, the female was clearly in the image of God along with the male (Gn. 1:27). The male and female together constituted the full image of God.

More specifically in Scripture the idealized image of the Wisdom of God was portrayed as the perfect housewife (Pr. 31:10-31).

It was the fall from the Garden of Eden, Scripture clearly explains, which placed woman under the dominion of the male, causing her to lose her rightful place as co-ruler and equal with him. Everywhere that the pagan male dominance exists, it is a sign of our sinful and fallen nature. The inferior status of woman does not symbolize a life "risen in Christ."

This Semitic tradition as recorded in Scripture of sensing feminine qualities as equal with the masculine and somehow incorporated into God continued most often in the Eastern, mystical and popular traditions of Christianity where heart knowledge has been as important as head knowledge. The Fathers who continued in the Semitic tradition also avoided the intellectual trap of consistency of symbol, a characteristic of the Hellenic and Latin traditions.

So in the East and in poetry, God could somehow be both male and female as He is often described with both masculine and feminine imagery in the Old Testament. As the prophet Isaiah said of Yahwah: "Like a son comforted by his mother will I comfort you" (Is. 66:13).

It is among these less speculative, more poetic, mystical or more heart-oriented, existential or Semitic-influenced Fathers you find suggestions of woman as image of the Holy Spirit, or a link between either the Spirit and the feminine or the Spirit and the feminine Wisdom.

Some References Among the Fathers

St. Methodius of Olympus, the third century bishop-martyr, was one of these who described the Holy Spirit with feminine imagery. A poet and a mystic, St. Methodius compared the Holy Spirit to the *costa Verbi*, the *rib of the Logos*. Methodius was not a speculative theologian, but lapsed into poetic rhapsody. Similar to the writer of the Song of Songs, Methodius wrote of the soul's mystical ascent, describing it with the imagery of love poetry.

It is also in the east, according to the Catholic theologian Father Louis Bouyer, that the Wisdom texts of the Old Testament were spontaneously attributed to Mary in the earliest Christian liturgies. The people instinctively confirmed an essentially feminine orientation of Wisdom.

In *Woman in Christian Tradition*, especially in his chapter "Orthodox Models," Tavard documents some of the hints of femininity in God found in the early Greek Fathers. Among these are the poetic flights of St. Ephrem of Syria who has been called the "Harp of the Holy Spirit." This Syrian saint described the Holy Spirit mystically or allegorically in feminine imagery, comparing the *air* or *breath of God* to a mother.

According to Father Tavard, it is significant that St. Ephrem was totally in the Semitic tradition, unaffected by Hellenism.

In my other researches I discovered the link between the Wisdom of the Old Testament and the Holy Spirit of the New documented by the Anglican theologian and Scripture scholar, Henry Barclay Swete. In the notes to his classic, *The Holy Spirit in the Ancient Church*, Swete points out that St. Irenaeus of Lyons, Pope St. Clement of Rome and Theophilus of Antioch identified Wisdom with the Holy Spirit. I also discovered the analogy of St. Methodius, who called the Spirit "the rib of the Logos," in Swete's translation of Methodius' writings.

Father Matthias Joseph Scheeben's comments in an appendix on the Holy Spirit in his *Mysteries of Christianity* introduced me to St. Gregory of Nazianzus' use of Eve's birth from the side of Adam as a possible example of procession, not by generation. This was during one Church Council debate when the Fathers were asking about the Holy Spirit, how could a Person be born, but not by generation.

None of these hints are conclusive.

They are clues, suggestions to help modern theologians in developing a much-needed theology of the feminine in God. As Father George Maloney, the

115

patristic scholar and director of John the XXIII Institute for Eastern Studies at Fordham University explains, "There are just sporadic references to the feminine in God among the Fathers."

These references are always mystical and allegorical, according to Father Maloney. They do not refer to women in the flesh. "Anti-feminism was a traditional thing of the Fathers. Women were the flesh pots, to be avoided," he says.

"It is only when you get into the commentaries on Scripture that they begin describing the feminine in mystical terms or allegorically. It is only when they get mystical or poetic that a few of them refer to God as woman or in feminine imagery," he said.

"There is a Season . . ."

It is only now in the late nineteenth and twentieth centuries that it appears that Christian theologians in the Western tradition are seriously searching for a theology of the feminine in God. Perhaps this is true because the concept of the feminine in God, or woman in the image of God, is an idea that has its Time.

The earliest stages of revelation history see the emphasis on Yahweh, the Father, with the spirit of God somehow linked in an indefinable way. The emphasis, counteracting the pagan fertility idolatry of that time, was on the One-ness of God.

Then later, nearing the end of Old Testament revelation, in the Post-Exilic period, the spirit of God somehow became linked with the Wisdom of God as a feminine figure. This emergence of the feminine Wisdom in Sirach followed a world-wide Wisdom movement which started in Sumeria around 2500 B.C.

Similarly, a world-Logos movement preceded the birth of Christ when the Greeks began talking about the Word or the Mind of God around 500 B.C. From the birth of Christ and through subsequent centuries the emphasis was placed rightly on the Lordship of the Son, the Divinity of Christ. Generations debated the reality of Christ, His Divinity. Church Councils and Synods argued the meaning of this God-Man. It was enough to defend the divinity of the Son.

Now it appears the times are again calling attention to the feminine and its necessary relationship to both the Holy Spirit and to God. The world-wide emergence of woman is part of this movement. So is the psychology developed by C. G. Jung, perhaps through a certain guiding of the Spirit, which is leading us to a greater appreciation of the feminine.

As C. G. Jung recognized the very real human need for incorporating the feminine into God, so the Roman Catholic Church has unconsciously acknowledged this need, first defining the Doctrine of the Immaculate Conception in 1854 and then the Doctrine of the Assumption in 1951. Aware of the psychological importance of this doctrinal development in Catholicism, Jung called the defining of the Assumption of Mary the most significant event in Western Christendom since the Reformation.

Not so coincidentally, the proclamations of the Marian Doctrines and the world-wide woman's movement have been accompanied by another breath in the Church—the rise of interest in the Holy Spirit. This began officially in the Roman Catholic Church when Pope John XXIII opened the Second Vatican Council calling for a "new Pentecost."

The Post Vatican II era has been a Time for revelation of the Holy Spirit in the Church. Undoubtedly it is also the Time for the revelation in salvation history of the feminine in its relationship to God.

Three years ago when I first started mentioning this concept of woman as image of the Holy Spirit, many were either startled or aghast. Now this idea seems accepted, almost naturally, when I speak of it. The concepts of the motherhood of God or the Holy Spirit as feminine have also been occurring more frequently in newspaper features and magazine articles.

Reaction was significant to a recent article by Leonard Swidler in the *National Catholic Reporter*, (31 January 1975): "God the Father: masculine; God the Son: masculine; God the Holy Spirit: feminine."

Several letters to the editor printed in the "Repartee" section of the paper repeated the standard theology taught about women or the all-male God in seminaries a generation ago. But several more revealed the growing awareness of a need to discover the feminine in God.

One particular letter, by Father Kevin G. O'Connell, SJ, who teaches Old Testament and directs the field education program at Weston College School of Theology in Cambridge, Mass., was most favorable. In it he wrote, "Thank you . . . for encouraging us to think of the Holy Spirit as feminine. This is a line of thought that I have found helpful for several years now. . . ."

In the letter, Father O'Connell described a frescoe he had observed in a tiny old church in

Urschalling, in Bavaria, built over 1,000 years ago, in which the third figure in the Trinity "had long brown hair and no beard, along with the clear suggestion of female breasts under the gown . . ." Father O'Connell's reaction reflects what Leonard Swidler (who is a member of the religion department at Temple University) describes as a "feeling in the bones" growing among priests, religious, laity. It is not a strictly rationalistic, hard theological concept, but an intuition, a flight of poetry: there is something truly feminine about the Holy Spirit.

This is a new movement in Western theological circles, a new current begun gently at the end of the nineteenth century and now expanding in ever-widening ripples. Out of the icy expanses of our cold rationalism and harsh technology a new season of the Spirit is budding with its promise of spring, the New Pentecost, a wisdom of the heart.

It is a Season . . . .

REFERENCES

Encyclopedia Judaica Jerusalem. New York: The Macmillan Co., 1971.

The Interpreter's Bible. New York and Nashville: Abingdon Press, 1955.

The Interpreter's Dictionary of the Bible. New York and Nashville: Abingdon Press, 1962.

A New Catechism. Trans. from the Dutch by Kevin Smyth. New York: Herder and Herder, 1969.

New Catholic. Encyclopedia. New York: McGraw Hill Book Co., 1967.

Sacramentum Mundi, An Encyclopedia of Theology. New York: Herder and Herder, 1968.

Sacramentum Verbi, An Encyclopedia of Biblical Theology. New York: Herder and Herder, 1970.

Scriptural references are from *The Jerusalem Bible* (Garden City: Doubleday & Co., 1966) unless otherwise specified.

BIBLIOGRAPHY

Alt, James. "Is There a Basis for Women's Lib?" *Know Your Faith*, XX (March 3, 1972), 1-3.

Achtemeier, Elizabeth. *The Feminine Crisis in Christian Faith.* New York and Nashville: Abingdon Press, 1965.

Bainton, Roland H. *Women of the Reformation, In Germany and Italy.* Minneapolis: Augsburg Publishing House, 1971.

Bardwick, Judith M. *Psychology of Women, A Study of Biocultural Conflicts.* New York: Harper & Row, 1971.

Blenkinsopp, Joseph. *Sexuality and the Christian Tradition.* Dayton: Pflaum Press, 1969.

Bordeaux, Henry. *Edith Stein, Thoughts on Her Life and Times.* Milwaukee: Bruce, 1959.

Bouyer, Louis. *The Seat of Wisdom.* Trans. by Rev. A.V. Littledale. New York: Pantheon Books, 1962.

Brenton, Myron. *The American Male.* Greenwich: Coward-McCann, Inc., 1966.

Bruns, J. Edgar. *God as Woman, Woman as God.* New York: Paulist Press, 1973.

Callahan, Sidney Cornelia. *The Illusion of Eve.* New York: Sheed and Ward, 1965.

Cervantes, Lucius F. *And God Made Man and Woman, A Factual Discussion of Sex Differences.* Chicago: Henry Regnery.

Congar, Yves. O.P. "My Maternal Hearth." *Sign*, Vol. 52, (June, 1973), 13-14.

Conley, Kieran. O.S.B. *A Theology of Wisdom, a Study in St. Thomas.* Dubuque: The Priory Press, 1963.

Daly, Mary. *The Church and the Second Sex.* New York: Harper and Row, 1968.

Danniel, E., & Olivier, B. *Woman is the Glory of Man.* Trans. by M. Angeline Bouchard. Westminster, Md.: Newman Press, 1966.

Dourley, John. "Carl Jung and Contemporary Theology." *The Ecumenist*, Vol. 12, No. 6 (Sept.-Oct. 1974), 90-94.

Evdokimov, Paul. *The Struggle with God.* Trans. by Sister Gertrude, S.P. Glen Rock, N.J.: Paulist Press, 1966.

de Fabregues, Jean. *Edith Stein.* Trans. from the French by Donald M. Antoine. Staten Island: Alba House, 1965.

von le Fort, Gertrud. *The Eternal Woman.* Trans. by Placid Jordan, OSB. Milwaukee: Bruce, 1962.

Ford, J. Massingberd. *The Spirit and the Human Person.* Dayton: Pflaum Press, 1969.

Friedan, Betty. *The Feminine Mystique.* New York: Dell, 1963.

Bibliography

Fromm, Erich. *The Art of Loving*. New York: Harper & Row, 1956.
Graef, Hilda C. *The Scholar and the Cross, the Life and Work of Edith Stein*. Westminster, Md.: Newman Press, 1955.
Grassi, Joseph A. "Is the New Testament Anti-Feminist?" *St. Anthony Messenger*, Vol 81 (September, 1973), 41-44.
Harding, M. Esther. *Woman's Mysteries, Ancient & Modern*. New York: G.P. Putnam's Sons, 1971.
Henry, Antonin Marcel. *The Holy Spirit*. Trans. from the French by J. lundberg and M. Bell. New York: Hawthorn Books, 1960.
Haughton, Rosemary. *The Liberated Heart*. New York: The Seabury Press, 1974.
Irenaeus, St. *Proof of the Apostolic Teaching*. XVI, *Ancient Christian Writers*. Trans. and annotated by Joseph P. Smith, SJ. Westminster, Md.: Newman Press, 1952.
Jung, C.G. *Psychology and Religion*. New Haven: Yale University Press, 1938.
Lederer, Wolfgang. *The Fear of Women*. New York and London: Grune & Stratton, 1968.
Maloney, George A. *The Breath of the Mystic*. Denville, N.J.: Dimension Books, 1974.
Maloney, George A. *Man, the Divine Icon*. Pecos, N.M.: Dove Publications, 1974.
McCarthy, Abigail. "The Motherhood of God." Commonweal, (9 August, 1974), 422, 439.
Montague, George T. *Riding the Wind*. Ann Arbor: Word of Life, 1974.
Morris, Joan. *The Lady Was a Bishop, the hidden history of women with clerical ordination and the jurisdiction of bishops*. New York: Macmillan, 1973.
Most, W.G. *Vatican II–Marian Council*. Athlone, Ireland: Alba House, St. Paul Publications, 1972.
Neumann, Erich. *The Great Mother, an Analysis of an Archetype*. Princeton: Princeton University Press, 1955.
Phillips, J.B. *Your God is Too Small*. New York: Macmillan, 1961.
Rahner, Karl. *The Trinity*. Trans. by Joseph Doncel. New York: Herder and Herder, 1970.
Scholem, Gershon. *Major Trends in Jewish Mysticism*. New York: Schocken Press.
Stein, Edith. *Writings of Edith Stein*. Trans. by Hilda Graef. Westminster, Md.: Newman Press, 1956.
Steinmetz, Urban G. *The Male Mystique*. Notre Dame: Ave Maria Press, 1970.
Stern, Karl. *The Flight from Woman*. New York: The Noonday Press, 1965.

Stuhlmueller, Carroll. "Women Priests: Today's Theology and Yesterday's Sociology." *America*, (December 14, 1974), 385-387.

Swete, Henry Barclay. *The Holy Spirit in the Ancient Church*. Grand Rapids: Baker Book House, 1966.

Swidler, Arlene. *Woman in a Man's Church*. New York: Paulist Press, 1972.

Swidler, Leonard. "God the Father: masculine; God the Son: masculine; God the Holy Spirit: feminine." *National Catholic Reporter* (31 January, 1975), 7, 14.

Swidler, Leonard. "Jesus Was a Feminist." *Catholic World* (January, 1971), 177-183.

Tavard, George H. *Woman in Christian Tradition*. Notre Dame: University of Notre Dame Press, 1973.

Ulanov, Ann Belford. *The Feminine in Jungian Psychology and in Christian Theology*. Evanston: Northwestern University Press, 1971.

"Woman's Day at the Abbey." De Pere: St. Norbert Abbey, Sept. 22, 1971.

Women in Ministry: a sisters' view. Chicago: NAWR Publications, 1972.

Wood, James. *Wisdom Literature, an Introduction*. London: Gerald Duckworth & Co., 1967.